THE STRANGER IN MY MIRROR

Athena Grace

The Stranger In My Mirror by Athena Grace

ISBN 978-1-952027-17-8 (Paperback)
ISBN 978-1-952027-28-4 (Hardback)

This book is written to provide information and motivation to readers. Its purpose is not to render any type of psychological, legal, or professional advice of any kind. The content is the sole opinion and expression of the author, and not necessarily that of the publisher.

Copyright © 2025 by Athena Grace

All rights reserved. No part of this book may be reproduced, transmitted, or distributed in any form by any means, including, but not limited to, recording, photocopying, or taking screenshots of parts of the book, without prior written permission from the author or the publisher. Brief quotations for noncommercial purposes, such as book reviews, permitted by Fair Use of the U. S. Copyright Law, are allowed without written permissions, as long as such quotations do not cause damage to the book's commercial value. For permissions, write to the publisher, whose address is stated below.

Printed in the United States of America
New Leaf Media, LLC
470 W Broad St #1276
Columbus, OH 43215
thenewleafmedia.com

Dedication

If you read my first book, "Definition of An Ex-Wife," then you'll enjoy my continuing adventures in "The Stranger In My Mirror." This is my yearlong adventure of everything new in my life—you know—without a husband?

Does life ever move forward after divorce? Will your daily activities really return to anything near a "norm" again? For me, it's been one adventure right in line with another marking step without my permission. The emotional roller coaster of Decision-Making 101, dealing with an ex who keeps changing the rules for child rearing, and every difficulty that I never thought could happen, has happened!

Besides, how does one deal with that "lonely gene" that was never there before, since your significant other is no longer around? I wish I knew! Besides, no one wrote a handbook on how to succeed and survive after divorce, or did they? I just know that writing down one's feelings every day has directed my emotional roller coaster that was once swept away with that final paperwork. It doesn't go away—even after your "freedom" returns. Now, the rules have changed, and we must conform to a new way of life or die trying.

So, now that you're free, can life get any better after your divorce? That's usually the question that everyone has in their heart after the "big day" when you get your "walking papers." I'm still trying to figure out that question—even to this day.

This book is dedicated to everyone out there going through his or her "next chance" at a good life that they so desperately deserve.

So, now join me now on my next adventure…

Table of Contents

Chapter 1	–	I Want My Mommy	01
Chapter 2	–	Now It's My Turn	15
Chapter 3	–	I'm On My Way – I Think	27
Chapter 4	–	Square one – Again	35
Chapter 5	–	Mother May I?	49
Chapter 6	–	An Ex is an Ex is an Ex?	63
Chapter 7	–	Dismount!	71
Chapter 8	–	Three, two, one…launch?	94
Chapter 9	–	I have arrived, or have I?	104
Chapter 10	–	Next Course, Please?	119
Chapter 11	–	Nap Time	128
Chapter 12	–	Reflections	143
Chapter 13	–	Go Forth and Conquer	157
Chapter 14	–	One Year Later	174

Acknowledgements

Life in general is hard enough but throw a divorce into the mix and you get "Life plus more pain." Besides, there is so much advice out to getting you to the next phase of your life, but does it really help? I really don't believe that God promised us a life of pain and anguish, but since it's here, guess what, we must move forward.

This first year after my divorce threw me more curve balls than I wanted to admit, but each day I had new challenges that were met and then overcome. So, I just wanted to share my thoughts in this book, and how I felt on life's lessons that challenged me through my entire soul.

Just remember this—together with one's friends and family, we can all go forth and conquer those bastards who have come into our lives and made us so miserable!

I Want My Mommy

I am reminded of a time long ago when I was about five years old at my grandmother's farm. I was running in an area with a lot of large rocks, and I just happened to find one causing me to trip. I hit my knee on a rock, and I remember the pain was excruciating. I was with my grandmother, mother, and aunt, when they heard me cry out, and they all came over to consul me. I distinctly remember my grandmother saying, "If you hold your knee really tight, the pain will go away." As my little tear-reddened face looked up at her, there was something in her voice that touched me deeply. Then, for just a few seconds, the pain did go away, and my tears stopped. But, alas, my pain came back. It didn't last for long, but at the time it seemed it would last forever.

I guess divorce is very similar to this incident long ago. The pain comes quickly, engulfs you, and makes you either deal with it, or it encompasses your soul. So, what will we do next? Do we listen to those around us to make us think that the pain really will go away? The answer lies in our decision-making skills and our own strength, I guess.

We can either choose success or we can choose failure. We can let the lowest point in our marriage totally destroy our life or we can get up, dust ourselves off, and point to a direction that will lead us to our destiny. We could also point with our middle finger—at the bastard who got us to this point—but what is our destiny? For our life, as we knew it, was "comfortable," or was it? Did it sometimes feel like you were stuck in a rut, but it was just easier to stay in that situation than leave it all behind? Plus, our significant other sometimes made our decisions for us, and we didn't feel like we had a choice—right? But, making decisions we once thought was impossible for us to handle, are now the ones we have to make whether or not we want to make them.

After my divorce last year, I was convinced that life would get better, and I would survive. Well, guess what? Life has a way of messing up so bad that you just want your mom to hold you and take the pain away. It's kind of hard to do that now since I live 1,500 miles away from her. Well, I must admit, she did offer me a place to live if I moved back to her house—in another state, of course. I'm 48 years old with a 13-year-old son. Why in the world would I want to revert to my childhood once again? I mean—things would fall back as they were when I was in high school, right? She would want to know where I was, at all times, and when I was coming home. Plus, now she'd have another question for me. Who was I dating, or on the flip side, she'd want to fix me up with someone. What a horrible thought! I'm sure she'd be asking me when I was going to find a new man—and this would be the question of the week! In addition, I would or would not have my son, since his father would have a cow if I took him out of state to live. He did make a comment, when we were getting divorced, that I would miss our son if I left. Jerk!

So, what was the straw that broke the camel's back for me—I guess it was the fact that he wanted someone else. I know I was miserable in that relationship, but I didn't leave. Why? I guess I don't really know. Maybe I wanted to stay for my son, finances, or even security—if that's what you can call it. I now look back and see this was not a healthy relationship and I should have left long ago—long before he cheated. It was inevitable since our relationship was so rocky. It wasn't a 50/50 connection, and that should have been my first clue. So, at what point do you just decide to leave? I think I finally figured it out after my divorce. You must be at a point where you're "done" with everything that's going on in your life, and you want something new. No one tells you this, and all your friends can harp on you that it's not healthy, but you can't listen to friends and family until you're at your break point. In addition, it must be your lowest point—ever! It's a hard lesson to learn, but I guess for me it was the fact that I had morals that kept me sane. I had always promised myself that if a man cheated on me or if they hit me, I'm gone, and for good! I never believed I had to put those values into effect in my life, but fate stepped in and shocked the Hell out of me.

After making that 'fateful' decision of confronting my ex with his extracurricular activities, I have found you must evaluate your situation and really decide if what you have now is right for you. For me, it was the correct decision to say goodbye, and I have never looked back, because I don't want that relationship anymore. No one deserves to have someone treat you that badly, and no one should put up with emotions that set you over the edge. I guess I was unhappy for years, but I just put up with it because it was "comfortable." But what is comfortable? Should anyone, male or female, be put in a position in a relationship that does not feel right for him or her? Well, that's a big NO! So, when does one grow a spine, and make a "command" decision? I guess no one can tell you; you must come to your own conclusion and say enough is enough!

Divorce presents us so many problems. Such as, if my son were to go with me back to my home state, with his father's permission, of course, there's the new school, and making new friends, and then I'd really be a "single parent." Plus, my hometown is very small, and the "word" about my divorce would leak out and it would be all over the place. I would hear whispers behind me when I walked by; I would be the "chosen one" in their eyes that would be seen as "the chick that couldn't keep her man!" Or would I? Would my friends from high school, and the people I don't know shun me? Would I be singled out and now ignored because I was "forced" to be single, and I would try to "take" their man? I'm sure it could happen in any town, big or small. Who put these rules into place anyway? I didn't cheat on my husband; he was the one who had wandering eyes and body parts that took him to the other side of the fence. I still feel like I'm being punished because now I don't live with anyone, and he does. So, does his current "family unit" count as a family? Is there such as thing as togetherness with any relationship? I don't have a significant other like he does, and by that, I mean they are living together, and I don't have a man in my house living with me. So, am I the one who's different now? I'm so confused!

As for my co-worker, Mary, she is still dealing with her soon-to-be ex. He keeps playing games with her and her kids. He's still not stepping up to the plate when it comes to his children. His youngest is also dealing with anger issues related to all this mess. Her oldest son has accepted the situation and wants to move on from this mess even though he doesn't like it.

This situation reminds me of a co-worker several years ago who had terminal cancer. When he died, he had two young sons—one was 11 years old, and the other was 9 years old. At the funeral, the oldest was holding together his emotions, but the 9-year-old just lost it. After the service, when his wife was greeting everyone who attended, her youngest was sobbing so badly, I was surprised he could stand up. My heart just broke for him. This happened years ago, and now these boys are now young men. I hope they have moved on with their lives without their dad being there for them.

Divorce is so different than death—in a divorce; that "person" is still around to deal with. A death is just that—a "death." You morn, you cry, and then life goes forward. Well, if you think about it, no one ever prepares you for a loss like that. Sometimes it's so unexpected, and it hits you like a lead brick that blindsides you so badly that you never get over it. The only difference between the two is that death makes the relationship final, divorce doesn't. So, what is the answer? I guess if I knew, I'd be the heroin of the day. I just want to know the answers, but they never seem to come as quickly as you want them. Having your faith, though, is one answer to believing things will work out. We do not know "His" plan, but our faith will get us through—one must believe that!

I guess losing a parent to death or divorce has its ups and downs. The one scenario is permanent and the other could or could not be permanent. The only difference is that when a parent dies, there seems to be more closure than when a divorce happens. In a situation of death, there is a grieving period and a funeral that brings more closure than a divorce ever could. Both scenarios are sad, but which one really helps you heal? If someone can explain that one to me, I'd love to hear it! It just seems that life sometimes presents you with lessons that take you to places you never dreamed of before. Can we survive? Sure, we can! Will it be painful—well, that's a no-brainer! Yes!

Even though I didn't choose the single life on purpose, I have to admit that I am happier. There's no one now to come home to who will yell at me for just anything. My pets only see my mistakes, and since they can't talk, in words that is, I don't think I will get into any arguments with them any time soon. When I have my "off weeks" without my son, I can go "party" with my friends. Gee, that seems weird now! I'm in my late 40s, and I'm starting to feel like I've reverted to my 20s. No one ever explains this to you after divorce, so why do I feel guilty now that I have my freedom? Before, I had a set routine. You know, washing, ironing, and house cleaning, plus taking care of my son with his homework and activities. I guess my world revolved around my family and I took a back seat to everyone—even myself. For some reason I didn't count in that whole world of a "family" unit. I even picked up after my ex—what the Hell was I thinking? That man is an adult, and just because he didn't learn any manners on the etiquette of putting clothes into the hamper and putting other things away properly, doesn't mean that I was the next in line to do it for him. The chick he's with now does the same thing for him—is she crazy? She'll get tired of it soon enough or she's an idiot for putting up with it. Also, I just found out that "he" didn't get the new chick anything for Valentine's Day—OMG! So, I see he hasn't changed. I didn't get anything for that special day last year either. I wonder what she thinks about that. He also didn't get our son anything for Valentine's Day, and he seemed a little hurt when he told me that. Did my son expect his dad to do anything? He hadn't done anything in the past, so why would he do anything since we're now apart? For, it was I who was the one in charge of that area, and I always said it was from his dad and me. Also, I was the one who went out of my way to buy Christmas, birthday presents for his family, and special days such as Valentine's Day and Easter. I guess I was the "chosen" one when it came to chores that got designated to me.

Well, with all the other things that divorce presents to you, things from the past seems to always haunt you. With me, it's about the house we had together. We had originally agreed that my son and I could stay in the house as long as I wanted since "he" moved out. I guess we didn't work out as many details as we should have, for now, he thinks I'm in charge of all the repairs and the taxes. Don't get me wrong; I do pay the mortgage, which is only fair. But, since we're both on the hook for the taxes and it's not included in the monthly payment, do we both acknowledge that we should each pay half? Plus, the things that were wrong with the house when he left seem to be my problem now—according to him. Perhaps, I'm at that point where someone should poke a fork in me, because I'm at the "DONE" part of my preparation. You know, it's the point when you really need things in your life to change for yourself—and you and only you can make it happen?

Personally, after being in this house eight months after I busted him, I'm really "done" with this set up too. I've changed so many things in the house to include painting various rooms and getting new furniture, but his "spirit" still lingers on in this dwelling. He has another home that he thinks he's responsible for now, and not this one, so I need to move on—besides, he has. This is the last thing that I want to have an attachment to with that idiot who will stay in my life for longer than I want. So, now that I've made that decision, what do I do next? For this house to sell, there are several decisions that need to be made such as splitting the profits or perhaps a loss. Or will he think since he took out a second mortgage on the house, and didn't tell me, that I should be responsible for that one too—well, that's a no brainer! Of course he will! It will probably get to the point that there will be several arguments before this is all said and done. There are things to fix, such as the broken windows upstairs, the broken hot tub, and the leaky dishwasher. This should be an interesting conversation, huh?

In addition to the house "thing," there's always other issues one must decipher, such as do I pursue a new love life, or do I become a nun? Sounds like a joke, but I guess it could come true. I haven't known any women who have done this, but probably some who wish they had. Besides dating again, I've known a few women who have dated again, and for some strange reason have chosen guys to date with the same names—and then marry them! Yikes! That's even worse than marrying the same guy twice who cheated on you! I've contemplated this issue and I can't judge all men as the one that just dumped me. But I hope that I don't find another man with the same name. I just remember years ago when I dated a guy named Doug who was a complete jerk to me. Then, a few years later, I had the privilege of dating another guy named, "Doug." It bothered me so much that I had to dump the second guy even though he didn't do anything wrong, just reminded me too much of the first one who cheated on me with my roommate. I guess I wanted to get him out of my life before "he" had a chance to cheat on me too. It was unfair what I did to him and yes, I can admit that now, but at the time it seemed like a really good reason. What a "putz" I was! It's amazing how we do things and what we think when we're in our 20s? Huh?

Plus, now that 20 years have passed, dating again has become quite complicated. Everyone seems to have so much baggage, such as ex-wives or even ex-husbands who are "nut cases." Or men or women whose kids are grown and they don't want to date someone who have children still at home or vice versa. Sometimes the opposite sex is just confused, and they don't know where they're going in life. I guess their next decision is "should they stay, or should they go on" with their life, and this seems to be in their next big decision-making process. Besides, some people had their children when they were younger than me, and now their children are adults. So, the question nowadays is, would their adult children accept me if I dated their dad? On the flip side, if your or their children still live at home, will they accept you because they want their parents to get back together? Crap! There's another thing a person must deal with in the "post-divorce" state. I had my son in my mid-30s, so I guess that will be something the new man in my life will have to deal with or he will have to hit the road. Life seems to be such a challenge at times, and right now this is the hardest challenge with which I'm now dealing.

My job is also driving me crazy! I work for a company that has increased its workload, but not its staff. What was once a pleasant place to work now has become a long eight hours a day. So, let's see. I hate where I live because it's not mine, and where I work, I don't feel like I can accomplish anything! Gee, I thought life was getting better—perhaps I was wrong? It seems like I can't get ahead. I just got rid of one idiot in my life and now the rest of them are lining up behind "him." This is all in addition to my knee problems—but surgery is just around the corner. In just over four weeks, I will be off for over a week recuperating. However, the workload will increase again while I'm gone. Now another project has been placed upon us and I won't be here to help out—just one more thing to drive people crazy. I so want to do something else with my life, but the economy has placed a huge burden upon anyone trying to find a real job and the pressure is more intense than ever.

I guess this is one test I will have to see if I can pass. Life seems to always throw you a curve ball, and if you don't have a glove that fits your hand, your chances of catching it are very slim. So, what does a person do to change their circumstances? Or will we ever know what to do? I mean, there are so many things that are "not on the table" when you get those divorce papers in your hands. Things such as finances, affecting every part of your being, seem to be number one in my book. I mean, think about it, how do you feed your kids when "he" was the breadwinner? Or do you feel guilty when your kids are with him because he can provide better than you? For now, you don't have to worry about what or how you'll feed them for those couple of days or week(s) when they're gone, because you can now save some money? Talk about a guilt trip to put upon yourself! Plus, what do you eat? Is macaroni and cheese or Roman noodles your meal of choice? There's also that can of soup in the pantry that can be heated readily—and maybe you can make two meals out of it. That's only about $1.50 plus your drink for one meal. So, now you're covered, but is it really fair to you too? The remorse factor seems to be constantly around you, and there's nothing you can do about it. For, at one time, there were once two of you with jobs, or in some cases one person worked, and the other one stayed home with the kids, but you still made the bills somehow. How is life fair now? It isn't! So, what are your plans to change your life? Is going back to school an option? Or do you find a different or a second job? A plan is what you need now, but how does one proceed?

Life never seems to be so complicated before a divorce. But now there are new changes happening all around you. If you shared the family automobile before this, do you still have to share it now? Do you have to work out other issues in your personal life in addition to divorce? Was your life in so much chaos before the "divorce," and now it's just another thing to throw gasoline on? Gee, where's a lighter when you need one? These things just seem to add to the mess of divorce. Plus, are some of your ex's things still in your home after he or she left, and you don't know what to do with them? I guess one's plan must include how to break free completely of that person. You are now a force of "One," but how do you do it when you have children? I'm sure it's easier without children, but right now, I can't relate to that reality. My little sister didn't have children with her ex-husband, and she recently told me she was so glad it happened that way. She was completely free of him, outside of seeing him in the town in which they both lived. With me, it's just the opposite. We have a son who is still a minor, so we both must constantly make decisions affecting him. So, getting along with "him" is quite the effort sometimes. Some of the things that come out of that man's mouth still amaze me. I know his decisions also astound the universe—so is someone listening? It's like reality and fantasy is intertwined somehow and he's confused, and how do I stay the strong one and keep quiet? Am I the only one who feels that he's an idiot? He probably feels the same way about me. Plus, it may only be our friends who know the truth about our plot.

Another indication that divorce has disrupted your life is when your ex won't take responsibility for his or her kids. They may live with only one parent, or they may end up sharing a week with your ex and a week at your place. In addition, some parents seem to take on more responsibility than others, or in other cases it may now "finally" be equal. The cheating parent may feel compelled that it's their time to "pony up to the bar," and prove they're the "accomplished" one. However, they are now trying to prove to their child they were right all along even though they were the one who cheated in the marriage. Others will still be the same lazy bastard they were before, and now they're still showing their ignorance of Parenting 101½.

So, if you're the one who's left with most of the responsibility to raise your children, what's your plan? The court system can help only so much, but I think it's your family and friends who are attached to the support system of whom you can trust the most. I know I've gotten so much support from my friends, since my family lives far away. My ex has even stepped up to the plate to help our son with his homework, and projects for school. Ouch! Did I just say that? I guess miracles can and do happen, but WOW it's still interesting when they do work out better than you thought.

With all the things you must deal with after a divorce, it seems you're back at square one with new and recurring crap that still seems to show up. For example, when I was going through the "divorce period," I couldn't sleep at all. All those hours of wasted TV shows in the middle of the night just added to my stress level. I so wanted to get at least eight hours of sleep each night, but my brain was so engaged with other worries. Well, guess what? I'm doing it again! I think I hear noises downstairs in the middle of the night, but it is just the guinea pigs in their cage clanking their bowls. Or it's the cat scurrying around trying to figure out if there is a mouse somewhere that he can attack. I've reverted backwards—what happened? Perhaps it's just the fact that I'm still in "our" home that he left? Or is it the fact that those memories are still here? You know, those thoughts that still remind me of where we had our fights, and where in the house we told our son that divorce was the only answer to our demise. The new paint on the walls, the new furniture, and whatever else I disposed of since my life-changing events didn't trash those memories I so desperately need to shed. So, what do I do now? Is selling the house and trying to find a new place to live my ultimate answer? At this point I don't know, but I need to have a response from my small prayers to the man upstairs—it seems to be my only answer right now. I need a direction, and God seems to be my only recourse to the decisions my ex made for me. I guess the one thing that really makes you wonder about your place in life is that there are no good answers. Because, each time I decide something, I wonder if I've jumped off the deep end of the pool that's not filled with water—only concrete. If the pool had water, it seems I could keep swimming down to reach the ring at the bottom that someone threw there, but I never seem to find it. Although I look everywhere, the prize doesn't exist, and no one can tell me where to look.

I hate to admit it, but I'm still scared, and nothing and nobody can give me the confidence I once had when I was single. Being married was a totally different state of mind. I mean, there you were, a couple that made decisions together;

at least at one time when you were together. But now, the tide has changed, and this time I have a child to take care of in addition to myself. At least when I was single, I had only one person to take care of—me! Now it's my son's education, schoolwork, preparing meals, etc., that must be addressed—the list goes on and on. I could, then, rely on my own finances for me and me alone. Now, I must watch every penny to make sure all the pieces fit in the puzzle. Do I feel resentful? Maybe a little, because now it's just me except every other week with my son. I have the responsibilities that I once had, but now it's different. On my "off" weeks, I have the freedom that "he" once had when he lived here. I can come and go as I please, which still feels a little strange. However, I am also in a big house by myself with no one to talk to and every sound at midnight and beyond startles me. Where does the game plan take me now?

Now It's My Turn

It's interesting what people feel and think after a divorce is finalized—at least on paper anyway. Life still goes on, but now everything is different. Each person now has his or her "new" routine; or his or her new set of "instructions" on how to proceed, and it's quite different from before. They are now involved and "existing" with new people. Each person has their own set of friends, or they make new ones with that new someone in their life. Plus, now they have a new "family" unit that extends beyond what they had before. So, what is the new plan for me? That question still lingers on, and each day is like starting from scratch because now your "ex" is not in your life as before. Decisions are still tough by yourself, but getting any type of satisfaction from each decision is something that still haunts me. Do I thank this person who did me wrong, or do I despise their actions forever and never forgive them? Should I hang onto his every move and feel like I'm getting the short end of the stick? Or do I move on and concentrate on me now? I guess it depends on the strength each person has when this situation happens. Some people can move on with no emotional strings, and others can't because they feel an overwhelming emotion that cannot be controlled by their own being. So, what makes us let go of those things that affect us the most? For me, it was the fact that I "forgave" him for his actions. I still don't know how I did it, but renewing my faith was what I believe was my first step towards moving away from that destructive relationship and continuing down a path that had my name on it. Believe me, I still think back to that day and wonder how I did it, and sometimes I forget that I forgave him, and I feel that hurt once more.

Looking back also seems strange. As I look at myself and at other couples, each of us has a different set of rules and responsibilities that we follow. In my relationship, I always seemed to be the one who was the most tired because I was so busy. I mean, how do you have relations when one person is exhausted, and the other is on their second wind? With one's job, the kids, the house and all the other chores a person does, I've concluded you can't do it all. That old saying reminds me of a commercial that aired in the 70s, when women were expected to bring home the bacon, fry it up in a pan, then please her man in the bedroom, in addition to everything else—so, who's got time for sex? After dealing with that many responsibilities, who has neither the time nor the inclination? Besides, there's got to be some resentment on one side or the other if a relationship is this disproportionate.

Several months have passed and the humiliation and disgrace involved in a divorce is still something I can't let go of yet. Besides, his entire family has rallied behind him, just as my family has stood by me. Even though, it was "he" who wandered from our marriage, it still seems his family still holds him in the highest regard. As for me, I have had so much support during this time, and now I have found out how much my family and friends totally despised him. I have heard such things as, "He never said anything nice behind your back," and "You were too sweet for him!" Ouch! What did I ever see in him anyway? There were so many warning signs that I ignored. For example, he told me once that he didn't have any romance left in him because of the women he had dated before me had treated him so badly, and now that "romance factor" just left him! Hello? Did the aliens take his heart? Or did he ever have one? This conversation happened just before we got married. So, what in the Hell was it that I still respected about him? What were the values he had instilled in his soul that made me still want to be with him? As I look back, it may have been his excitement for life or his wanting to constantly succeed.

He really did have a zest for life, but as the years wore on, he seemed to "try" a lot of things, but none of these plans worked to make him rich. Yes, being rich was his goal, and to this day he hasn't made it there—at least monetarily. I mean, I wish him luck, but why is this a goal that someone must obsess about? What is implanted in a person's psyche that makes them think that money is the root to all happiness? Sure, it pays the bills, but true happiness must come from within. You must be happy with yourself before you can be happy with someone else—well, at least that's the way I feel. As for him, I don't think he's truly happy about anything. I'm not rich in a monetary way, but I can pay the bills. I believe it's what I hear from a church service that really lifts me up to the point that I feel really satisfied with my life. I hope one day, he will get to that point, and maybe his new girlfriend will get there with him. Personally, I think that if they went to church together, they would feel better about their lives and they would have a common goal. But how do you make your life change when you're stuck in a rut and you don't allow yourself to find the ladder to get out of that hole?

I even heard a message reiterated in church this morning that really hit the nail on the head. The Pastor spoke of one's desire for conceit and selfishness. It's a way of life that God does not desire for anyone, and if a person continues down that path, God will call him or her out. I guess it's that "karma" thing that eventually comes back to haunt you when you least expect it when one chooses a certain way of life. As for me, I wasn't raised to believe that I was better than any person. However, once when I was young, I remember I got a little cocky one day and said something about my brother. I compared him to someone who had developmental disabilities. I thought my dad was going to backhand me. From that point on, I started to understand that I needed to treat everyone with respect and realize that they, too, are allowed to express themselves even though I don't agree. Perhaps if everyone did this, life would not be so complicated, or am I still in a dream state?

My desire for a new life seems so strange—I'm in uncharted territory and I feel very alone. "Our" house is now on the market and keeping it clean is quite the chore. Besides constantly cleaning it, I am also looking for a place to live if this house sells quicker than I expect. I even got a St. Joseph statue and buried it in the ground. It sounds quite silly, but he is the patron saint of your home and burying it upside down in your flower garden, facing the street, is supposed to be the answer to selling quickly. Trust me; ask any realtor or a Catholic bookstore and you'll see that glimmer in their eyes. I tried this at our last house, but only after seven months of it not selling. I buried him in the ground and within three weeks the house sold. Superstition is something I'm used to and if it works, so be it! Right now, I need all the help I can get so that I can move forward. I'm not Catholic, but boy does that Saint ever do good work!

Even the guy I'm dating weighs heavy on my mind. He lives about 40 minutes away, and we talk every day, in addition to seeing each other when we can. Our future is not determined, but we may still make it together. We've been through a rough patch, and I thought he was gone forever, but fate has brought us back together again. So, who knows what will happen now? He's very important to me, and I want so much to perhaps make a life with him. Sometimes, it seems we're in two different worlds, but somehow, we've made it this far. I think we just need to take each day as it comes, and then go from there. It's almost like we're both going through our own, but separate, mid-life crisis. I thought, at one time, that a mid-life crisis was just that—a once in a life time event. However, the older I get, the more I realize that a mid-life crisis seems to occur whenever and wherever it feels like it and, yes, more than once in a lifetime. It seems to happen around your 30s, then your 40s, and every decade after that. Did someone change the rules and didn't spread the word to everyone else? Or did someone say that life should be difficult as a game of chance? You roll the dice and fate will decide your future. Then you must guess what your next move will be. Do I go to jail and not pass Go just because I failed one of life's most basic lessons such as marriage? Or do I try this dating thing again and eventually marry once more? A good example is that I have two female relatives who have been married four times each. I also have two friends who have been married three times each. How did they make it from their first marriage to now their third or even their fourth? Where was their strength to do it all again and again? Besides, how did their children deal with that much emotional trauma? Geez, too many of these questions make my head hurt—how about yours?

I even went onto the Internet tonight and read some blogs from people who have been divorced. Most of them had the same issue—being alone again and now trying to trust another person in their life. It seems we all need and want someone in our lives, and when that trust is gone, for whatever reason, we must start all over again. That's where the hard part starts once more. So, what is the right time for each of us to start anew? I guess it's like the same question we have in our minds when we know it's time to leave that relationship. We must be at a "done" point in our lives. But, please, no sticking forks into each other to test this theory, ok?

So, in our "afterlife," what do we do to trust again? Do we let our guard down just for a second to feel those shivers down our backs when we kiss that special someone? Do we hold hands and walk down the beach with the ocean breeze flowing through our hair and remember our teenage years? Or do we drive down a winding road with the top down on that new convertible with that special someone beside us. Some things can make your youth come back with one thought of that special person, but it never seems to last, especially when we have been hurt so badly.

I guess there's something inside each of us that makes us want to feel exceptional inside, but getting to the point of saying, "I love you" again to someone scares the "heebee geebees" out of us all, right? Besides, how do we know that this new person won't treat us just like our ex did, and will they bring their own baggage to the table plus your own? The most extreme scenario, in my opinion, is a medical condition that can hit you or your new significant other so fast that it throws you for a loop and you question your sanity. Do I stay with this person, or do I drag them down with me when I want to protect them? The idea of a "relationship" brings up so many responsibilities. I guess the question is, when you have that special someone sharing the ups and downs with you, at what point do you expect them to be there for you? Next, do you feel guilty that you "dragged" them down to the bottom of the well with you because now they can't escape without some kind of emotional trauma? Besides, Lassie isn't available to save you. So, what is the answer? Do you dump them because you can't deal with your own emotional disaster, or do you give them the option to come with you? I guess it's one of those questions that destiny must decide. It's like that old saying, "What will be, will be." Sounds like a bunch of hog wash to me, but I guess there's some realism in there somewhere! What do you think?

So, just consider this, you got married in your 20s, 30s, or even early 40s. Then, you're married for a few years and for some reason it doesn't last. Now, you're in your mid-to-late 30s or even 40s—so how do you start dating again? Let me guess; one of your married friends wants to fix you up with a guy or gal who has a "great personality." They bring up the "personality" thing because now this person isn't as "cute" as they once were in their 20s. They may be overweight, be crabby because they were once dumped, or there's some other reason they can't get a date by themselves. Whoever came up with that crap? Wasn't that the scenario when you were single all those years ago? Your married friends wanted to introduce you to their friend, because they couldn't stand to see you single. Now, your married friends, or perhaps all your divorced friends want to do that dirty deed to you all over again. On the flip side, most of the people you hang out with now are divorced, and all they talk about is their ex and how bad he or she was to them. This would want me to stay single for the rest of my life. But why should we? Didn't God make woman for man because he was lonely? Who knows? All I know now is that the dating scene is quite different than it was before all this mess started. I don't feel the pressure now from my mom to "get married" because she doesn't want me to be alone into my golden years. I think she wanted me married back then so that she could have grandchildren. If I had a quarter for every time that that woman wanted me married, or when I told her I was dating someone new, I would have been rich in my late 20s, and I wouldn't have to find a man to keep me financially stable. Now, all she tells me, almost a year after my divorce is she thinks I should have just lived with my ex! Is this woman on drugs? Did the aliens take my mom and insert a different-thinking brain into the same body? Where was she all those years ago? Moreover, why did she put so much pressure on me to get married way back then? Possibly it was her generation that just dealt with life, and everyone expected you to get married. Divorce wasn't the answer in any scenario in her day. But maybe it was her generation that taught my generation to think differently. If you look at my cousins, I can count at least seven of us who have been divorced for some reason or another. I find this quite strange, since the generation that raised us to never get divorced basically taught us to not put up with crap that marriage could spawn. Holy Cow Batman! What were they thinking?

Another thing I've noticed after my divorce is that my habits have changed dramatically. I no longer feel that I "have" to watch TV to escape my circumstances, and on the weekends, I used to wear sweats and T-shirts for the most part. No longer! For some reason, I now hold myself in a higher esteem than I did when I was with my ex. I dress better—now it's sweaters and jeans on the weekends, and I also want to clean out my closet and get rid of those T-shirts that I don't wear anymore. I think I let myself get into a rut and I didn't respect myself anymore because I was so miserable. I let my ex be number one in my life, and I let him degrade me. At least that's what it feels like now as I look back. Everyone should count; especially me! Damn it! Why did I let a person that was my "soul mate" take me down to the bottom of a barrel and leave me there? I have more respect for myself now, but then, I guess, I was under a spell that lasted way too long. Respect is something that should never leave you—whatever the circumstances! I've come to the conclusion that each person will act as they see fit, but you should never let that other person "control" your entire being.

So, where do you go when you're at the bottom of the barrel? I guess finding that point is everyone's responsibility; however, no one seems to know how to show you the way back to the yellow brick road. A therapist can direct you; your friends can console you, but you and only you can make that decision to go forward. I guess what makes us get up and move first thing in the morning should be the thing that gets us off our butt to change our position in life. But that motivation is different for everyone, I guess. There seems to be more of an incentive to go to work, but not to proceed to an area of our lives that seems so distant. So, why are we so scared to tread in unchartered waters? Is it that we don't know the outcome, so we stand, as far back from the cliff as possible so we won't fall off again? Maybe. I guess my conclusion is that we're too scared to walk the "same" walk as we did before because it hurt too much the first time. So, our goal is to not stray from that path again. But will these footsteps truly be the same as before? The trust factor seems to really haunt us, I guess, to the point we no longer want to feel that insecure. However, are we really secure in our past lives? Since divorce was the ultimate outcome, where did the tide turn and take us out to sea and leave us without that precious life preserver? Life seems so complicated sometimes and it's like Maslow's Hierarchy of Needs. Self-preservation is at the bottom of the pyramid and if the need is not met, this can make us feel insecure in ourselves. We must be able to breath, have food, water, sex, and sleep, to fulfill our physiological needs. It then moves up to safety and security, love and belonging, esteem and confidence and then self-actualization, which includes morality, creativity, problem solving, and a few other things.

    I guess the thing that really floors me is that we must have such basic needs to get to the other things that we can't function without. In addition, every man in my life, both past and present, has seemed to go on with their life without me. Maybe it's just me, or is it that men over 50 are so busy they can't or don't have time for me? I've dated two guys now after my divorce, and while they are very generous to everyone else, they seem to let their personal lives go by the wayside. Are they too busy taking care of everyone else in their life, such as their friends and family, that they neglect the most important thing—a meaningful relationship? Are they trying to avoid this part of their life because they haven't dealt with what they really desire? Have those "demons" been lurking in the back of their heart for so long, from a bad relationship, that their current situation of being alone feels too comfortable for them? Who knows? I guess my next question is, "Do they really want to deal with their past and, more importantly, their future?"

I've also noticed, since my divorce, that men either want to jump back into a relationship rather quickly because they need a "mother" figure in their life, or they avoid a relationship because the Black Death will soon sweep over them and "kill" them off from reality. One example I can remember is that I knew a guy who worked odd shifts at his office so that he would have an excuse not to date anyone. Then, get this; he worked at this job for 5-6 years after his divorce! Talk about denial! I thought that was a river in Egypt—who knows, I could be wrong? I've even known women who've been divorced for more than five years and swear that they will never get married again. So, what's the answer to our dilemma? If I knew, I would be rich and everyone who has gone through a divorce would want answers from me.

I even wonder why men think the way we do sometimes. I guess that's every woman's innermost thought. When they say they will call you later and they don't—what happened? Are they not adults like us? Why do they not follow through? I guess women can do the same thing, and on that note, I think our idea of not calling is somewhat different. We're usually trying to avoid "that person" so they'll go away. I truly believe men either get busy with something or "forget"—yes, "forget" to do what they say they will do. Sometimes, they're just trying to avoid doing the inevitable. Don't get me wrong;

when men and women don't want to do something, especially in a relationship, we all make excuses. I've seen it happen, and I've also participated in it too—so, I'm just as guilty.

It's the same in any new relationship. When "he" or "she" says they will call and they don't, isn't our first reaction of mistrust? Do we think, especially after a divorce, that this new love in our lives is seeing someone else? Or, what other burning questions go through our mind? Those old feelings of doubt are never far from our minds, and they come back rather quickly. So, how do we get passed these feelings and trust someone again? Perhaps the world will never know, but it's in our nature—men and women want that special someone, right? Everyone must be a glutton for punishment, I guess. But don't we all want to be needed, and want that passion that makes us feel good? Or are we crazy for thinking that way? Why would we ask for that kind of pain all over again? One might think we all nuts, but I've spoken to women who have married for the second time, and they've told me that this one was much better than the first. I guess there's hope, huh?

I'm On My Way - I Think

The road ahead seems, as rocky now, as what I just went through. But, once you're divorced, stuff seems to keep happening and the crap that comes out of your ex's mouth can still amaze us. I guess "our" way of thinking never seems to be as "pronounced" as theirs. Do we all gravitate to our own whims, and is everything we do so perfect and their way so totally wrong? At this point—who knows? So, how should our lives be different now? What pulls us in one direction or another? Now, I see my friends differently who have gone through a divorce within the past year. For example, a former co-worker is now dating a guy with the same name as her ex-husband. Ouch! I don't think I could do that—too many memories of "him" would be there. Also, one of my co-workers who was divorced last year has now gotten remarried. Another continues to date the same guy and they're still very happy. As for Mary, well, she continues to struggle with her ex. They're still married but have been living separately for months. Both have not moved on with their "separate" lives.

They haven't even filed for divorce yet either. Why? I'm sure money has a lot to do with it, and the changes taking place between the two are what bring them together. They still share a car, and still live rather close to each other. I keep trying to convince her that she needs to move further away from him and closer to work. She needs closure so badly, and a few others and I, think it would be a good thing for her and her boys to be as far away from "him" as possible. She needs a fresh start, and this is one way for her to move on without that "same ole treadmill" she currently has in her life.

    I guess the question now is how much longer do you dwell on that past relationship? Plus, how do you move on without him or her? For, it seems something always draws you back and you constantly must deal with that person. Whether it involves your children, finances, or something else, they never seem to leave. Sometimes it would be better if someone got a magic wand and made them disappear. Unfortunately, no one has one of them. Also, when do you stop fighting with that person who made your life so miserable when you were with them? Plus, now that you're not together, why do you still want satisfaction for what they did to you? Is there still a part of you that wants revenge because they cheated on you or ruined your perfect life together? For me, I seem to want him to feel as bad as I felt not so long ago when I "busted" him in his endeavors with another woman. Will I ever be able to go my separate way and never have to deal with him? This probably won't happen because we have a child together. I guess there will always be a part of us we cannot throw in the trash can and then run the other direction. So, what is the answer now? Can we really heal our hearts and minds and really focus on our new lives? I just wish I knew the answer. It hasn't even been a year since my ex left and I know life will never be the same. I still feel I'm strong in so many ways, but there are times that make me wonder about how much strength is left in that "half-full" glass. Why do I question myself? I guess it's in our genetic makeup, or at least in mine. Strength seems to come in spurts, and in others, the calm and stillness in our lives seems to be shaken like an 8.0 earthquake. During that event, our whole world is shaken, and then after the calm, we're awaiting the next quake to scare the crap out of us once more. We always seem to be on the edge waiting for another event to occur. Will we ever be the same, since we are always on the edge, and trusting our surroundings will never be the same?

Now, here comes the part where life gets interesting. The chance for me to be together with someone again is coming up soon—I know it's out there. So, do I jump at the chance to be with another guy, or do I put my life on hold just to please my son since he thinks no man deserves my attention? I mean, he likes the new guy in my life, but how much is he really going to accept me being with a new man? Also, can this man's children and mine, or even our friends, really accept our new lifestyles? I once had a male friend whose dad had died a while back, and now his mom was now dating again. He was very hesitant about her getting hurt once again and he wasn't very acceptable of her new life style. I guess he wanted her to be happy, but deep down inside, he thought this new guy would leave her penniless and heartbroken. He was very protective of his mother, and as her son, he should have thought this way—I guess. I never knew what happened to his mom because my job transferred me to another state, but I've often wondered about that situation. As for my own mother, after my dad died over 9 years ago; she swore she would never marry again. She said that she had put up with so much crap from him that she didn't want to get married again. So far, she has kept that agreement with herself, but is she truly happy not sharing her life with someone who could really make her life complete? Is she missing out on life because of what she has chosen? Besides, she has other family members and friends there to help her, and even though I live so far away, I often wonder about her life. She says she hears noises in the middle of the night which frighten her. Plus, there is no one to wake up to in the morning. So, what part of "lonely" does she not understand? Personally, I want to share my life, again, with someone. Because I know there are men out there who are caring and perhaps could be my "soul mate" –my real soul mate.

Now that I've been on my own for several months, I've concluded that you're never really at that point where you can let go of everything in your past marriage. There will still be things you will fight over with your ex, and there are things that will haunt you because you don't have the answers to the questions as fast as you'd like. Some people will dwell on these two things forever, and others will try to distance themselves from that timeframe as quickly as possible. So, where am I right now? I guess I'm at a "push/pull" timeframe. I keep trying to go forward, but something seems to always draw me back a few steps. But how do we really distance ourselves from our "former" life? How do we let go of our "failures" and the "failures" of our ex? Will we ever think good things of that person who cheated on us? Will we always have our guard up when we meet that new and exciting person who has swept us off our feet? There are so many questions to ponder, and I think I'm getting a headache trying to keep my head above water.

Well, about break ups, I have a former co-worker who was divorced over 15 years ago. She is now living with a new guy, and deep down inside she still can't fully trust him. So, she makes sure that all the expenses for her home, etc, are in her name and not the new guy's. She even has a back-up plan to protect herself just in case they break up and he says that part of the household expenses should be credited to him in the end. Wow! Have we come to a point in our lives where our every move is being watched, or are we watching our own moves? Another friend, Leslie, who just lives down the street, has finally made her move. Her alcoholic husband just lost his job, and once again this has put her over the edge. Perhaps my advice helped; maybe it was just her time to heal; who knows? So, she has made the decision to move out of their home and leave with the kids and get their own place. After initially looking into apartments, she now has "ammo" to run with her decision and to make plans for her next steps. She reviewed her finances and realized that she could make it without him. Especially since he doesn't have a job—once again. He has been such "dead weight" for her for so long—all the drinking binges, the lost jobs and no ambition to look for another one. I know she can be free of his dependence upon her. So, what will he do? Who knows? The house will go under and with him in it. She so desperately wanted to have a total family unit, but how does that work when one family member fails to uphold their end of the bargain? After speaking with her last night, I feel she has renewed her strength, and her future is being made for her by her current actions. I'm proud of her for taking a stand. Even Mary told me she wants to file for divorce by the end of March. I hope this time she can do it. I mean, we both found out about our ex-husbands within one week of each other, and I've now been divorced for six months. Her paperwork is getting stale on her dresser. I guess it goes back to the old saying, "You can't lead a horse to water."

It's interesting that we all have our own time frame for success or even failure. I guess it's our makeup of what we hold near and dear to our hearts. I've seen it before, we can put up with tragedy upon ourselves, but put our children into the mix, and then others around us will see another side of our soul. I always like to think of it as, "Hell hath no fury like a pissed off mom!" It even happens in the animal kingdom—get a female animal who's young is in danger of being hurt or killed, and boy, you're taking your life into your own hands. You've seen it, right? Of course, you have. But animals only have one way of looking at things—survival of the fittest. We, as humans, have a little more to think about and most of it involves money. Too bad we can't look at life without it, but we're stuck. From what I've seen, money can be the root of all evil, but it's also the ingredient that holds everything together. The scariest thing is that most of us need help from a partner to financially survive. With that in mind, the Bible tells us that trying times will come into our lives, but they will pass. Is this our "test" so that we can understand that everything in life is a trial and not a God given right? So, what are we clinging onto that we can't let go of? Especially in a divorce situation? As the Pastor explained one Sunday morning, we can never experience the fullness that God has for us if we're not willing to let go of that emotion that has us so tied down. We must pour it out of ourselves in order for us to let go of our burdens. So, let God take care of our burdens and we can then heal.

I just remember that first church service I attended last year when I was going through my divorce. I held it together well during the service, except for a few tears, but leaving the church, I just lost it. I guess it was that event that really made me realize that I wasn't Wonder Woman, and I couldn't deal with this all on my own. I have learned to let God into my life so he can take control by changing my mind and my heart. Learning to live in a world surrounded by chaos and despair is a lot easier when you have a little help from the guy upstairs.

This last year has been such a challenge for me and certain days seem to creep up from behind and attack me when I'm not looking. A good example of this were the events of this week. I'm off work due to my knee surgery; so, what's on my mind? Well, if you must know, I'm getting anxious about my current situation. Yesterday I looked at two apartments to see if they would fit into my budget. In addition, the house is on the market—no takers yet, but I know it's just a matter of time. I've had four showings of the house thus far, and since the school year is almost done, I'm sure I'll have a buyer soon. My world seems to be turning upside down. I'm scared again since my future is so fuzzy. The guy I'm seeing is requesting his job transfer him to an office closer to me, but he's waiting to hear something from his supervisor to see if he can transfer. So, what will happen? Guess what? I don't know the answer once again. I just feel so lost, and no one can rescue me. I want to cry, but the tears won't come; I want to scream, but I don't think my vocal cords are working. I even looked at a condo today, but unfortunately, my bedroom furniture won't fit in the master bedroom. Besides, it's a short-sell, and I'm not comfortable with that situation. Because suddenly, I'd be in a situation where I'd probably have to shell out thousands of dollars to fix something and I don't have it.

I don't like feeling this vulnerable. It's not my demeanor, so why is it happening? I guess I'm still in that "uncertainty" period of my life after divorce. "He" has a new life that he chose with someone new; so, the other half of his life is complete—or is it? If you look at it this way, he went from my bed to hers. When we were together, I was lonely—even though he was here, and I'm still lonely even though he gave me my freedom back. I so desperately needed freedom from his control, but it's weird having it. Is having another person in your life the fulfillment you need? Besides, when do you decide to marry again because you have gotten to the point of trusting that so deeply once again? Dating is still so foreign for me, and being close to someone new is still scary. I just wish I had training in this area of my life that was part of that "pre-marital counseling" I should have gotten just before I got married to my ex.

4th Chapter

Square One – Again

I guess I just don't understand my newly found freedom. At one glance, I'm back at square one because this was thrust upon me—I didn't choose this life—he handed it to me. On the other hand, I wouldn't have it any other way. I just hate him for making me choose this life that I currently live. This week, especially, has been hard. I'm bored out of my mind since I'm off work and must let my knee heal. I guess I just have too much time on my hands and my mind is working overtime. Can life be just a little easier than this? I mean, I say my prayers to the man upstairs for a direction, and lately I've gotten some answers rather quickly. I've asked where I need to be in this life, and thus far, I've put my house on the market, gotten knee surgery, and my new love is working to get closer to me. I should be thankful, and really, I am. I guess I don't have much patience; I just want things to happen quicker.

I want to recover from this 'illness' since I've supposedly been on the healing path for nine months now. That's long enough for a new life to be born—at least from a female womb anyway, but not from a catastrophic event, right? Well, no bombs went off; no shots were fired, or were they? What really happened? Sometimes, I let myself be so vulnerable that I look back and ask for answers that never really came. Sometimes, the word, "failure" comes to mind. But who is the real failure here? Is it because I don't fit into a "family unit" now? Is it that my ex obviously has someone to complain to, to love, or to be with? Besides, am I denying myself of a life that still may happen?

Boy, today just had to end lousy! For the first 12 years of my son's life, his dad's priority was himself and as he put it, "paying the bills." It's amazing that the last two years have changed. His priority is now his son, and even a little adjustment in any doctor's appointments is life threatening. I guess that's why he's my ex…what a jerk! My medical issues come in second to my son according to my ex. I had to readjust my son's appointment to get in my appointment and you'd think the world had come to an end. Right now, I hate this man with my whole heart and soul. This man, who once held me as an equal to him, now thinks I'm the scum of the earth. Well, guess what, he's lower than that in my book. Plus, "he" always held himself above everyone around him and he made his wants and needs a priority over anything else. Now he thinks the world should stop for our son. So, what happened to his brain? I guess he's trying to impress everyone around him and make sure his son doesn't become a burden to him when it's time for our son to leave the nest. For, he always said he was going to leave the U.S. when our son became of age. Personally, I hope he doesn't let the door to the airplane hit him in the ass when he leaves. I'm just so mad now that I could just spit nails! On the other hand, I hate feeling this way; it's like I'm losing control of my being, and I don't like that. I'm really trying to keep it together, but today is not one of those days that I can control my actions. I don't have my emotions in check, and I don't know my direction right now. I just feel so lost and confused once again, and now the tears are coming too easily for me. My strength has taken a vacation and put me on notice. My vulnerability has resurfaced, and it has made me a wreck. I need my strength back to carry on with my life and right now there's no one to cling to that will make me strong. My anger is getting the best of me, so what is to become of me? I haven't felt so alone and scared as I do now. I need a good, strong hug, but if I don't get it, tomorrow is another day; I hope. I'm glad I have a lot of tissues.

Today, I'm a little better. Boy, what a meltdown! I knew that a day would come where I'd have too much on my paper plate and it would start to leak. I guess I can be strong when my health is good, but when I'm vulnerable, I'm a goner. Today, I got the stitches taken out from my surgery scars. Another trip down south to the Army base to get them removed. As I look back, I'm glad to have had the opportunity to serve my county, but on the other hand I see the military as disorganized as it ever was—even back when I was on active duty. There are good points, though it's a "hurry up and wait" atmosphere there.

As I look back today, I am reminded of an organization (aka…the military) that thrives on change, respect, and doing a job that has to be done. All the uniforms, military-issued boots, and haircuts are all an indication I still belong to an organization that is alive and well. Don't get me wrong, I really did enjoy my time in the service; it was just the other issues that brought me to where I am today. I was married when I was in the service, and when I was to be deployed to another part of the county, my ex (husband at the time) refused to go with me. He didn't support my interests even then. He was a civilian and was bound and determined to stay in the state where we had gotten married. It just so happened that I didn't go because at that time I was trying to resolve the issue of my current knee problem. I was eventually honorably discharged due to a medical condition, so the subject of me getting transferred had ended.

I guess I still wonder what would have happened if I had been transferred to a different state. Would he have remained faithful, even back then? He hadn't met "her" at that time, so would it have been someone else? Besides, would he have blamed me for fooling around on him? I guess there's so much stuff to this divorce game. There will always be questions about when, why, and where an ex did what they did. In addition, do you blame yourself for what your ex did? As for me, I don't blame myself entirely. Of course, we both seemed to go our separate ways. We both changed over the years—and sometimes not in a good way. Our ambitions and goals split into two different paths. He started to not believe in God; as for me, I still believe to this day and make Him a part of my life. I guess I really need that feeling, you know, the one that fills you up and gives you hope for the future. I don't think I could stand not knowing there's an entity out there that will be there for me when I'm down. It's a shame my ex doesn't see that need.

I guess when you're down—from things not under your control—one's mind creates crap to sink you even lower. For example, I had a dream last night that involved me being at a zoo. I was too close to a crocodile, and he tried to attack me. I ended up winning the battle by killing him, but then a myriad of animals, from bugs to bigger animals, attacked me. I woke up before the end of this dream feeling so scared and alone that it was hard to get back to sleep. Was it the fact that my current relationship is faltering? Do I see it ending once again? At this point, "yes" is my answer. Well, I got my answer today, Easter, of all occasions, he said goodbye once again. He did this before on Valentine's Day. Boy, does he have lousy timing! Besides, why did I let him do this to me once again? He thinks we are too different because he is Catholic and I am not, and he lives too far away from me. Personally, I think he's just making excuses for not wanting a relationship. I once told him that I didn't believe he had dealt with his past relationships. It has created a problem for him, and he can't move on and be truly happy. Well, this time I'm truly done with a capital "D." Maybe it's just me, because I'm not into games. Whatever he can't deal with in life shouldn't be my problem, right? It's like the men in my life; over 50 years of age, can't or won't let themselves be happy. Do they really want to live like that? Or have they become so stagnant in their lives that they are more comfortable in their new mold?

I guess my new goal is to take care of me. I'm so tired of caring about a guy who's not putting forth what I'm putting into a relationship. So, here goes my new purpose. I'm going to stop thinking about what could happen for me; and I'm going forth towards my own goals and not looking back on my past failures. For, in my past relationships, I've put too much thought into what could be between us. I was thinking "twosome" I guess. Now, I'm thinking "Number One." I have no choice.

Even in church this morning the Pastor said that it's only God who can make you whole—not a relationship. Don't get me wrong; being with someone who makes me feel important is something that I want, but I must put God first and then take care of me. Sure, being dumped for the second time and by the same guy (within just a few months) hurts, but what really is going on? Is fear of commitment the theme? He even said once he was afraid of being alone for the rest of his life—so what gives?

Commitment seems to be a topic for the ages. With the divorce rate around 50 percent, it seems "that" word is taboo. So, why then do we even get involved with any significant other? There's another one for the record books, right? I guess life has a way of ticking us off so bad sometimes, that we don't know where to go from there. The pain of a relationship that goes badly does teach us something, but at this point I don't know what it means. So, are we better prepared for the next relationship? Sometimes the answer is yes, but not always. Being wanted and having a sense of belonging is something we all strive for, but unless we're strong in some way, the "dumpee" is always left alone somehow. However, I think we all want a chance for a new relationship somehow.

So, if we learn from the lessons from our last relationship, even if it ended poorly, why do we desire to do it all over again? A relationship that has just ended may leave us feeling lost and all alone once more. Emptiness can haunt and overwhelm us to the point of sadness and despair. The hurt can consume us to the point that every part of our body and soul hurts. Our interests that once devoured our thoughts are now put away for safekeeping. The future that we once dreamed of is now gone and no hope of love is looming anywhere close. We seem to second-guess our thoughts and actions. So, what are we going to do now? How do we overcome our fears and hopes of what we once thought we wanted and needed? I wish I had as many answers as possible for the questions that I've thought up lately. Maybe then and only then, the hurt would go away and stay in its special place with all the other bad things in my life. I guess I'll miss everything about that relationship, but what can I do? Too many irons were on the fire during that time and, I guess, the distance was the last straw. It wasn't my idea to leave. I wanted it to work, but he couldn't deal with me not living closer to him. He was also Catholic, and I wasn't—big Whoop! So why did we even try to be together? He has a different belief system than me, even though I am religious too. He doesn't believe a lot of what I think is ok, so will I ever give him another chance to come back into my life? Probably not…I've given him two chances thus far. I don't think my heart can stand any more hurt from his actions. I just need to hold back the tears from his decision.

This up and down emotional roller coaster is driving me crazy. Why do I put myself through this crap and why do I let my guard down? I even talked to a friend of mine who's been divorced for years now. She said that she and her ex constantly fought over trivial things that included their daughter. Their "knockdown, drag out" fights were overwhelming at times. Now she can look back years later and just remember those words and talk of it in a past tense. I still have several years to go before I can say that. My son is still a minor and I have at least four more years of torture from my ex to deal with before I can really let go of his words and torment.

I even looked up on the Internet today about narcissism and I think I his picture should have been there. His traits tortured me over the years. His backstabbing started by him ignoring me—for he gave all his attention to others, but in private he constantly put me down. I even found out this information after he left, from our friends and neighbors who told me stories. He would say bad things about me, while beefing himself upwards. He showed little feelings for my well-being; often I had to fend for myself in a lot of ways. Most of the time I felt shame, hurt, humiliation and I was powerless to do anything—and for so many years. Perhaps that is why I stayed with him for so long—my strength was frozen in time. It was only after the last 10 years of this abuse that I finally got enough stamina to stand on my own. Just remember a narcissist is one who never feels they should be questioned because they are always right. On the other hand, they can also be very charming and highly praised for their work ethic. In addition, this type of person can fool those around them by taking charge of situations and "being an expert" at any subject—and quite convincingly.

Although a lot of people did see through him. Because I was often asked how I could stand him, I would reply with, "I just ignore him." What the Hell was I thinking? Relationships should be 50/50, right? Well, it shouldn't be like that one I just left; which was 80/20, and I was the "80." I was blind for so long, and I often feel I was cheated out of my right to be happy. There were often things that I wanted to do, but with his lack of encouragement, I dismissed a lot of what I wanted to do with my life because I felt he was right. For example, I wanted to go to school for different things, but each time, he told me that I wouldn't make any money doing "that." So, I would quit and look for another way to find myself. So, now as I look in my rear-view mirror, I feel like I should start all over again and he doesn't. I feel like I was cheated in a way because he was always "right" in his thinking—and I allowed him to control me! Ouch! What was I thinking? Plus, when he left, there was no waiting period for him to ponder finding that someone new. There was no period for him to morn over a love lost—he went out and found another love interest while he still had me! What a bastard! Will I ever recover from this? I surely hope so—in so many ways. I have my sense of self, but I also have a part of my heart that has been ripped out of me a few times since my ex left. I am now left sad, depressed, hopeless, and tormented by all his actions. However, I do have my freedom back and my sense of pride that took a vacation so long ago.

Moving on to my current situation, I guess I was expecting this man to say goodbye again. He kept hinting about the distance between us, and how we could never see each other because he was so busy. Lately he had to check his calendar to see what he had to do next. Then, he also said he had to attend a class out of state for six weeks. All these excuses were subtle, but I understood where they were going. He did this a few months ago, and I was familiar with his tactic. So why did I let it happen again? I guess I wanted to be with him; we were good together. We often thought a lot alike, we could read each other's thoughts, and we had the same values. Unlike my ex, our relationship clicked. I hate to admit it, but I thought he was my soul mate. Finally, I met the guy I was supposed to be with forever; at least I thought I had. I can't let this happen again. If he wants to get back together by sending me text messages or e-mails, well, it won't work this time. My heart hurt too much the last two times he did this to me. I really think if he wanted to be with me permanently, he wouldn't let the "distance" thing be the reason. There's got to be another reason he can't commit. I can't figure it out. There's something mysterious about him that makes me stop when I want to be in his world. Well, if my house sells soon and I move, the only way he can find me is via my cell phone. I could change it, but what would that prove? If I really wanted to disappear, what would it take to do that? I could get an unlisted, unpublished phone number, but that probably wouldn't stop him. Several years back, I had to do that since a boyfriend in another state was trying to find me. Boy, that was spooky. He was so obsessed with me, and I had to discourage him, and it did end up working. But, you see, I don't want to discourage this relationship. I just want it to happen naturally, or I must let it go. When we were together, we were good together, but when he went off the deep end, nothing mattered but us being apart, and the conversation stopped between us. I must concentrate on my son and myself now. I can't think of what it could have been, because there's nothing left to say, I guess. The last time this happened, his daughter asked him if he liked me. His response was, "yes." Her reply was, "Well Dad, you screwed up!" At least I had someone on my side. The strange thing is I never met any of his friends or family. Was it the fact that he was afraid of his friends and family liking me too much that he was "stuck" with me? Or was it the fact that he is Latino, and I am White? Big Whoop! Like I said, there's something that he is hiding from me, and I still don't understand his reasoning.

Well, it happened, guess who's trying to get back into my life? That wasn't too hard to figure out, huh? A text message from him one day later just about set me off. It was as if nothing ever happened the day before. I'm so tired of his wishy-washy ways in this "relationship" of ours. Well, my comment back wasn't nice, and I think I said something like he needed to find someone who was the same religion and who lived closer to him. I also told him that when I do finally move that I should perhaps change my phone numbers so that it would be easier for him to let go. Was I being too harsh? At this point I don't think so. I've dealt with him by saying goodbye and hello to me four different times. Why I put up with it is beyond my thinking now. He's an adult, or at least I thought so, but who's the scaredy cat now?

It hasn't even been a whole 24 hours since I sent this e-mail. It makes me wonder what he's thinking now. Besides, it was his decision to let me go, and then try to come back into my life—now the decision is in my hands. The emotional trauma I've felt has really affected me to the point that I know now what a teenager goes through—since I've obviously forgotten at this point in my life. The mood swings, the feelings of loneliness and the despair are all present. Gee, it's like going through a divorce all over again without the paperwork. I know he has never resolved his past relationships that have hurt him so deeply. We once talked a lot about what happened to him in those relationships that ended with his ex-wife having an affair. I just wonder how he handled it. Did he just shove his emotions to the side, get angry, and then suck it up? Did he yell or scream and then throw her out? Besides, did he ever get any counseling for his feelings? Somehow, I think he has never healed from his battle scars, and now that I have shown up, he's not sure what to think or even what to do about me. Like I said, we were good together. Maybe in another lifetime we could have been soul mates, but I think too much has happened for us to ever be together. Sounds like a sad movie that ended miserably, huh? I just hope he will find himself one day and realize what we had together could have been real, but without hard work and support from others, it was not to be. Am I sad? Of course, but I can't let a relationship that was going nowhere let me fail as a person.

I must believe that everyone, me included, deserves a lifetime of happiness, and if I don't find it in one place, it will be located in another. It's like looking for Easter eggs. You know they're somewhere near you, but you're not sure where to look. Besides, if someone told you where to look, it's up to you to eventually find what you're looking for, right? Besides, when we're not even looking for that special someone, they sometimes find us very easily, but not as soon as we'd like. We can never give up hope, be destitute in our thoughts, nor throw our hands up in the air. Unless one has given up a relationship for good because they refuse to date anyone, there is hope. All we have to do is believe that the right person is out there for us.

Now the question is, "What do I do now since the last two relationships haven't worked out?" In a way I'm dealing with boys whose ages are in double digits and begin with number 5. In addition, there is a different mentality that I'm coming across, but nothing like when I was a teenager or in my 20s. There's so much more to deal with now. There's still the pressure of making that first impression, that first meeting, and that first look when you first see one another. So, why do we as humans act like we do? Have we all been inbred? That's a scary thought, huh? I guess we never get old when it comes to relationships and wanting the best for ourselves. In a way, we should never settle for second best, but should we ever compromise our principles for one another? I believe we should be true to ourselves, and if compromising makes us into a person we don't recognize, then we should re-evaluate our way of thinking. In the end, this can cause us to shatter a relationship with someone whom we wanted to be with—but is it worth compromising our principals? Changing our way of thinking and doing is something a teenager would do—not an adult—or am I confused?

As we age, we become more of the person we, perhaps, wanted to be when we "grew up." But there's a "growing" period when we leave our parents. We can either become the person our parents want us to be, or we can go down a different path. But when we take those tools, we have been given, it doesn't always guarantee where we want to end up. However, hopefully these tools will lead us down the path to choosing a partner that we want to commit to forever. Sometimes we choose the wrong person for whatever reason, and we are in a divorce court before we know it. Plus, it's a sad decision that will follow us to the next life we choose. We are frightened, unsure, and sometimes rejecting everything we once stood for as an adult. We want to strike out, hate the opposite sex, and perhaps think that we will never find that special someone ever again. The isolation of being alone haunts us daily despite our friends and family being close. We want to share our lives with a special someone, but we are hesitant. The only ones we can truly trust and expect no changes from are our pets. That special dog, cat, guinea pig, or whatever never seems to be in your home are glad to see us when we get up, or when we come home from work. After feeding them, they are content and happy. They are non-yielding in their faith to us, for they accept us for who we are, not for what they want us to be. In return, all they ask for is love, affection, and sustenance.

All our relationships should be so simple—no constant expectations, no changing minds, and no grief. We should want to be together because we complement one another. It shouldn't be based on what one person can do for the other, in an unequal relationship. It should be an equal commitment during fun times, shared moments, and just spending time with each other. That would be too much of a dream, I guess, but it's a nice thought. I don't think I've ever been in a relationship like that. But could my dream someday become a reality? I guess it's possible.

It's interesting to know that when your crystal ball is in the shop that life goes on without you, and without your permission. You never know what things will happen when life throws you a curve ball—especially when you're not looking. Then, there's the idea of meeting new people who will influence your life and accept you for who you are. But life becomes a challenge wherever you are on that journey. I have met so many people lately through my friends and through a dating service after my divorce. It's been fun, but still, I'm cautious in my struggle to become a whole person. So, what is our desire and what drives us to get to where we're going? Damned if I know! I wish I did, but would life be as exciting then? Probably not, but I must keep in mind that whatever happens to me will be from the Will of God and from my next adventures. I want so much to know these answers, but right now I must live as if today was my last day on earth. I must make the most of what I have been given and go from there.

Mother May I?

So, now that I'm "free," where do I go from here? The decisions are still tough, the days still seem long, and the future is still a question mark. So, where do I stop to ask for directions? Besides, each new guy I meet is in his own arena—their guard is up, and I don't think they realize their actions. Everyone, at my age, also seems to have their own baggage and their own direction. Thus, I cannot let someone direct me with all their might, for I need to find my own way. It's like being a teenager again where I have to make my own mistakes, for a second time, in order to learn from my actions. Ok, who changed the game plan so that I have to revert backwards and become an adolescent once more? I'm not sure I like that scenario! I don't think my "adult" handbook contained this information. Plus, I'm not sure when everyone around me starts telling me, once again, what is good for me, and that I should start listening to their advice? Sometimes, or I should say a lot of the time, it's tough being an adult—let alone being a kid again. I think I want to start all over and go back into my mother's womb and hide from the world.

I even talked to my little sister last evening and she is within two weeks of having her baby. She's 40 years old and just starting a family. She jokes about being a "Geriatric Mom." I know there's some truth in that statement, and she's scared of what the future will bring. I have a teenager—so what's the difference? I guess I'm at the end of my parenting skills—at least until my son goes off on his own. She's just beginning the parenting process! But, if you really look at it, instilling values into your child never goes away. So, what's worse? Is it changing diapers and making bottles, or is it dealing with teenagers with diarrhea of the mouth? I guess moms all over the world were right when they said, "I hope you grow up and have kids that act just like you!" No statement has ever been more correct than any words from any parent. I guess teenagers are God's punishment for having sex. Sounds pretty accurate sometimes, huh? Life throws you so much at once, and sometimes we need more than a catcher's mitt to grasp it all.

I even had one of our volunteers from work, who is a very wise woman; tell me something today that really hit home. She said, "If a woman makes herself too accessible to a man, she's a goner!" I guess I never really thought of life like that, but my marriage was all that and then some. So, do all relationships have to be like that? I hope not. She even told me that her husband had cheated on her years ago. Why is it that almost every female I work with lately has been in a relationship where their significant other cheated on them? Just off the bat, I can count at least seven women of which that this has happen to, and I have worked with them at the same company! OMG! What has this world come to for divorce to rear its ugly head so often? It's a wonder that relationships even form and people want to be with each other as a couple. Am I crazy or what?

Is the "loneliness factor" coming into play to where we need one another at all? Do we all have such hang-ups in our past that we can't go forward and thrive? I just know that I miss my prior relationship with a man who couldn't go forward from his past experiences. I want to be with him terribly, but I know I can't, nor do I want to be devastated again. He must resolve the demons that have haunted him for so long or he will never find "Ms. Right." I only pointed that out to him because he obviously hasn't seen that reality in many years. What he does with that information is up to him to process and digest, but can he do it? I certainly hope so; he is a good person and deserves to be happy.

Just remember this, everyone is truly special, and we each deserve to be treated with respect, and not be controlled by that significant other in our lives. We should appreciate that special person, and never take advantage of them, right? I guess it's a battle of wits, for we have to keep our dignity and our common sense about us. For, it is this skill that keeps us truly alive—both physically and emotionally.

I really want to have a special relationship again, and with that in mind, I will not "settle" for a person who cannot figure out where they are going in life and how to get there. I've met men in the past who have said they knew where they were going; they just wanted someone to go with them. Well, it turned out that this man was so comfortable with his current life; he had no time for me. Don't get me wrong, he is a wonderful guy, but in my opinion, he needs to prioritize his time. When time becomes more valuable to someone than it is to their significant other, Houston we have a problem! I guess one's priorities are something that comes with an individual's territory. He even told me that after his divorce, he worked the night shift for several years to avoid a relationship. Who the hell does that? Is life that short that you want to avoid being involved with a significant other? You might as well go to a deserted island and live with the fish and the palm trees if you want to avoid people. So, where do we humans go from here? Do we become nuns and monks, or do we just suck it up and go forward? As for me, I vote for going forward.

Hey, remember in my last book I wrote many things about my co-worker, Mary? Well, good news to report, she finally, yes FINALLY, filed for divorce! She told me this on Tuesday, and I was thrilled for her. She even had the divorce papers served to him. Wow! It's been a long journey for her, but after 10 months, she's finally gotten up the courage to do what she's needed to do. I think now she has taken control of her life. She is even planning to move closer to work, and further away from her ex. As for me, I've been divorced now for almost seven months. That doesn't even seem real to me. This entire last year has really been so exhausting, frustrating—you name it, and I think I've felt it. I've had my ups and downs, and my emotional state has run higher than I ever thought it could run. I've had to make decisions that I never dreamed of making. However, I'm still standing strong; at least today, and I want to continue my journey to my next life. My friends and family are still there as my comfort zone and my support system. I don't know what I would have done without them.

So how do we get from one relationship that blows up to one that works? I'm still trying to figure that one out. The first guy I met after my divorce seemed so perfect. We got along in every way possible—it felt as if I had met my soul mate, but it seemed that he wasn't "ready" to commit. He had two prior marriages where "she" cheated on him, and he's never dealt with those emotions—even to this day. So, why hasn't he gotten over this? I wish I had the answer. It happened to him in the early 90s; it's now 2010; where is his logic that he can't see we're right together? He even commented once that if he had met me before I had married my ex, that we'd be married now. So, why can't he understand that I want to be with him—for real? It seems he keeps making excuses for us not to be together, and he's tried to end our relationship on a couple of major holidays. It's happened three times now—Thanksgiving, Valentines' Day, and now Easter. Yes, I allowed him back AGAIN! Is he afraid that if he spends a holiday with me that he has "committed" himself to me? Commitment has two meaning in my life—being together and being locked up—wish I knew what his definition was at this point! Has he let his guard down to where there's no turning back? He has come up with a lot of excuses why we shouldn't be together, but where are the reasons why we should be together? At this point, I don't know where to proceed. I sent him an e-mail stating that I really miss him, but it's his turn to figure out where he wants to be in life. Will this work? At this point, I don't know, but I am hopeful. The future is still to be written, and I don't think I have the pencil to begin writing the words. Either way, I must fend for myself for where I want to be in my life. I will not let him drag me down.

It's amazing how time messes with your mind. The more time that passes, we either get over our past relationship or we long for the one we know we should have had all along. We want a person who can make a life commitment with us. On the flip side when we've had a little too much to drink, we can long for what we don't have in our lives, and whimper over a glass of wine when we don't get it. I question myself for wanting to move on with someone else, but when you know that you're missing out on the "one" you know is right for you, it's hard sometimes to take that first step. Damn him for not wanting me! Is he afraid that I will hurt him like the others? For some reason, I think so; he keeps putting up his guard when I get too close. I know it's true because he has never dealt with the hurt that has engulfed him for so many years—he admitted it to me. I just wish he could understand that I'm not here to hurt him, but to complete him. Time will only finish this story, but I am not the one who needs to open the first page and start writing.

When it comes to my story and the story for the others around me, I seem to be writing more pages to this saga. For, today I got another jolt. My neighbor, Leslie, told me she finally decided to leave her husband. She found an apartment to lease in June, and so has he. It's now April, and she can't wait to leave her current situation and come to a commitment of containing her sanity. As for me, I have found another place to live; but only if I can qualify for this new townhouse. I'll be thrilled if it works out. The first time I looked at it, I was captivated. It's in a nice location and since the bank owns it, I may get a good price on it. I hope that I will find out good news this week. I need a change; I cannot stand staying in this house that my ex and I owned together. There are too many memories here that need to go far away from my sanity. I need a fresh start, and I hope this is my new commitment to change. Besides, he started his new memories, now it's my turn. I will say my prayers tonight and at church tomorrow—my address needs to change.

I need a change so desperately. I want a place of my own so that I can move forward with my life, not continue down the path from "his" old life. He made his choice to leave; now it's my choice to proceed with what is left. I can't rely on anyone to help me now, and I can't rely on my past relationship to make my future clear; for, he no longer exists, or does he? I am on my own now, and I should be able to make it by myself, right? I feel like I can't accept help from anyone, but with God's support, I will make it. It's my prayers that sustains me.

I guess it's the way a person deals with their past life that gives them a future direction, but you must make a plan. It starts by involving your outward side and your inward side being the same. What does this mean? Well, the Pastor this morning hit on something that really had a lot of meaning. He was referring that people should act the same in church as well as outside church. If you ask me, that's hard to do when you're going through a divorce. God wants you to forgive your ex, but how do you really, deep down pardon them? I had asked for directions to forgive my ex, and it seemed to come in about three weeks—yes, only three weeks had passed, and, in my heart, I forgave him. It was the higher authority upstairs that helped me; I just know it. I wish Mary could forgive her ex. I have often asked if she wanted to come to church with me, but since she lives several miles away, she has politely said no. I guess the one thing that really hit me in today's service was the statement that said something like God works good in us. Then it pours out of us the same way, and what comes out of us can be pleasing to him.

Boy, if we all could forgive and forget, we could get a lot further in life. We could live more productive lives and perhaps leave the past in the past, so we can move ahead with our future. I guess that man upstairs instills in us small changes that eventually lead to big ones to convert us into the person we were meant to be. A good example of this is when my divorce was final. I was approached by one of the volunteers in my office and he said to me, "I can tell you've changed. You're a lot calmer now." Wow, when did that happen? Was I that tense to where I was unapproachable to others? Did I convey an essence that told people I was that unhappy? I guess I did, because it happened with another co-worker that I don't see very often too. I guess we change and grow at such small intervals after a catastrophe that we can't see the changes taking place in our own life. I guess the "good" was stuck inside and now it was available for all to see. It seems other people around us can see us more clearly than we ever could see ourselves. I guess the word of the day is to be grateful for what you have, never second guess why things happen as they do, and to remove our emotions in these times. Then we won't have anything to complain about, right?

Just think if you remove a light, darkness will abound in one's world. But, if your light shines so desperately to where you need it in your life, it will expose the darkness to the ones who are lost and looking for answers. Wow, where did that inspiration come from? Sometimes the words just flow from my fingertips, and I have no idea where they came from! I guess it's like finding yourself all over again. It is a great mystery to some people, but for others it comes easy. Sometimes you go through tragedy for a very long time, and sometimes it's a very short jaunt to the corner store. However, we tend to deal with our emotions and our quests for the next life, which will never be given to us in a textbook—unfortunately. However, we must make plans and go forward as we haven't in the past. It's scary believe me, I know—I'm there! Every day is a challenge with the decisions I must make. I'm not even sure if I have the same shoes on sometimes, let alone socks. Then, preparing lunch for my son, clean clothes for him to wear—the list goes on, but my mindset is one that could be my downfall or perhaps it could save me somehow. It is my choice.

It's now Monday; the start of a new work week. Today is especially exciting because I am putting an offer towards that townhouse. I can't believe I found a place that I can afford by myself! I guess this is one more hurdle that I must cross and probably the most important one in my new life. I'm proud of myself for even getting to this point. All the worrying and concern for my future is heading down that golden brick road headed towards Oz. I guess I now need to hang on to the handlebars because this road can be a little rocky, but well worth it. Here we go—one more ride down life's path of sanity. Or should it be called, "insanity?"

With life's little challenges and the big ones too, one can never be ready for what life brings. As for me, I'm awaiting the outcome because another offer may be on the table too. So many questions go through your mind such as, "What if I can't really afford this place?" and "Can I really do this on my own?" I don't know why I'm questioning myself again, but here I go down that path of uncertainty. Why does life have to be so complicated all the time? Everything now seems to be a waiting game for me because I still don't know where I'm going. Will I ever know the answer? I guess that's the "million-dollar" question these days. Because I'm taking everyday minute-by-minute, it's amazing how my strength and sense of calm is at bay now. The only distraction is my teen-age son; he distracts me when I'm on the phone and when I'm on the computer. I don't think the male gene knows what to do if a female is busy doing something other than interacting with them. Don't get me wrong, I love him to death, but when his little mouth doesn't stop moving, I'm ready to put his nose in the corner. I guess the same goes for that significant other in one's life, at least the one you want to be with. They drive you crazy to the point of no return, but you love them none-the-less. So, how do you keep a calm balance? Boy, if I knew the answer to that question, I guess I'd be rich. My best guess is to keep a smart balance between you and your kids and your time alone. You must meet somewhere in the middle where you're both comfortable. I'm not a psychologist; I guess I'm just using my own interpretation of how things might work out best.

So, as we deal with those trivial issues of our current life, we always seem to put our life in reverse to revisit the past. It seems as if the hurt feeling of being dumped never goes away. Or, in some cases, bad luck seems to follow you wherever you go, and getting passed the "divorce" part of life is harder than ever. Take for example, Mary, today she tells me that her car got broken into, and her ex is dictating when he will give her more money. He has now gotten to the point where his finances are better than hers, so he has used that to his advantage. He takes the kids when he feels like it and for how long it suits him, and then he brings them back to her. There is never a routine to their "arrangement." So, I guess my question to this "divorce" thing is why does it seem like one party gets the "best," and the other gets the "worst" of a split?

Can someone just give me a handbook of answers to these divorce questions so I can follow it to a "T" to keep my sanity? The struggle is quite interesting some days and the people around us seem to be dragged along with us on our journey. They see the triumphs and tragedy, and even though they feel for us, they can't fully understand our grief and our trials in this life—if you can call it a "life."

I seem to be a little more stable in my struggles, but my friends and co-workers who have gone through a divorce or are currently going through one, are one step behind me and some are struggling for air. As for me, I didn't get the townhouse that I had put in a bid for yesterday. But that's ok for now. I don't have to move. I just want to get into a new place to save my sanity.

My goal is to get rid of those memories that have haunted me for so long. You know, those ones that still linger in each room of this house that won't go away? All those fights and reconciliations that go back almost nine years, and all of the tense moments that made me feel like a stranger in my own home. I guess it's easy to revert to those days, but I must refrain from making that move. For, I could get stuck there and never be able to put one foot in front of another. Thankfully my conscience will not allow me to go there now—at least I hope so.

I guess for some people, it can be harder than for others to move out of a relationship that lasted for too long. The circumstances involved in a split are the straw that could make or break a person, I guess. Time will only tell when life moves on. Besides, it's our destiny to carve out our next chapter from that block of ice. It could look like crap when we're done. Or it can look like a beautiful swan ready for flight, it's our choice.

It's interesting to see when one door shuts, another one opens. Well, guess what? This evening, I found another townhouse for sale; it is a brand new one for less than the one that I had originally bid. Go figure? The complex is trying to close out their town homes and I just happened to catch them at this point. The original price compared to the other one is around $20k less. Wow, what did I do to deserve such a deal? I guess I shouldn't second-guess myself; I think God just pointed me to the other side of town in a good area so that I can be safe and sound. Someone is watching out for me; I just know it! I have a call into them so I can check it out; I'm ready to jump on this or I will miss out on my chance to move forward.

I keep finding my way through this dense forest of mine, but for Mary, not so much. I think I finally figured out why she is so down. She sees her ex getting to do and go where he wants and when he wants. Plus, he just bought a new vehicle, which didn't help either. So far, she hasn't done anything to completely change her situation. Even though he has made several little changes, she still sees her life as if this didn't happen. All would be well if things were the same for her, and now she can't move forward from that thought. I know she needs to make plans for herself instead of dwelling on his life, but she's having a hard time accomplishing that task. I wish I knew how to help her.

On the other hand, she asked me how I felt when I looked at my ex's current life. I guess she wanted to know how I view the things he has and the things he does that I'd like to do but can't. I told her that I immediately get off that "idea" and think about myself, and what I want to do. Or I think good thoughts of things that are going right in my life now. I mean, what else can you do? I didn't realize that divorce creates another problem, the one that starts the race to have a better life than your ex. I'm not sure who fired that first shot to start that competition! Besides, who snuck that little secret in the "Divorce" handbook and didn't tell me?

Dwelling on these negative thoughts takes a lot of energy. I guess it's like frowning all the time; it takes more muscles to frown than smile, right? At least, that's what I've always been told. To this day, I've tried to keep myself busy with my friends and family so that I won't go crazy thinking about my ex. It's just that many thoughts always seem to run through the minds of us "normal" people who got the shaft. For our daydreams give birth to several things we'd like to do to them to make them as crazy as we get sometimes.

I truly believe our family and friends are the angels who are there for us. As for me, I try to make time for the people whom I didn't make time with before, such as my friend Marie. It's amazing how you find out things you've never shared before when you truly put forth an effort. I've known her since 1996, that's almost 14 years. Tonight, we shared things from our past lives, which we never knew about each other that made us laugh. You know, enjoying the times in your life that are special, tragic, and ones that just give you joy. As for my ex and I, somewhere, there was a part of our lives that we really enjoyed sharing together. But something went tragically wrong, and we both didn't fully commit those words to each other in front of the minister the day we got married. I guess we thought those words were ones that would last forever; boy was I confused!

I guess the best way to really get over those horrid feelings I had, and probably still have, is to really direct my attention to future goals and ambitions. As I look back now, I often wondered what I wanted to do in my life, but I felt he stopped me? What did I want to achieve in my life, but I felt it was better to take care of my family first? Finally, what did I feel that I gave up when we said, "I Do" and what part of me has always felt empty? These questions still thrive in my life, and I'm still wondering if I will get to the top of that hill to get to the other side. The struggle seems to never leave me, even though I am stronger than most women I know who have been through the same thing in the past year. I guess there will always be regrets of things not accomplished—but what good will it do me now? Well, that's a no-brainer! Nothing! However, I can't change the past, so I can't revisit that road, or can I? If I do, I must learn from those mistakes—not to dwell on them.

I still have days that haunt my strength. So, where to next? Damned if I know! Marie even stated there were things that happened in her previous marriage over 20 years ago that still disturb her when she thinks back. I noticed, when we talked, that she could think of those thoughts for only a few seconds before she came back to reality; you know, 21st Century. WOW! It's amazing how our previous lives can still come back to haunt us no matter how much time has passed. Sometimes it would be easier if we had short-term memory loss—at least for some things. Alzheimer's disease is looking pretty good right now. But would it really be easier? Have we grown due to our past experiences? Of course, we have, but going through it at the time seems so tragic and it feels as if it will never end. After some time has passed, things may get better, but there's never a set number of days, weeks, months, nor years that can really mend our soul. I think we're going to always be careful of our next relationship and our trust factor will always be in the back of our mind. I hate that fact, but I know it will always be there

An Ex is an Ex is an Ex?

So, when does your "ex" really become your "ex?" It seems like this person with whom you once valued so much in your life, has become an anchor weighing you down into the depths of an ocean so vast and wide that you can't even fathom your next move. For example, I want to buy my own place, and the home we had together, at one time, is the last thing we still must resolve. Well, maybe I'll figure it out; I'm so ready to leave this place that I currently call my home. I guess I'll keep looking for a place for me, so that I can really move on and "really" get him out of my system. Once I move out of this place, I think I will be free of his grip—I just can't take it anymore. There's still a part of him that has me captive and I don't like it. These walls have kept me a prisoner for so long; it's now time to move to the next avenue of my life.

Speaking of the ties that bind you, I have a co-worker, who is still in the same house she had when she was with her ex. But now the financial obligation belongs to her, and he has no ties to it at all. Then, the other day when we talked, she told me that she's been divorced for two years now, but her ex still thinks he's linked with her still. The reason I brought this up is that her ex called the other day and wanted her exercise bike! What was he thinking? Does he still think he can come into the home they had together and take what he wants? Besides, isn't there a time limit on possessions, and on how long the statute of limitations lasts after a divorce? To me that would take a lot of nerve to think you can still interfere with your ex's life in that way. What an idiot!!

It's also interesting how other people act who have gone through that "divorce" part of their life long ago. I went out with some friends tonight and one of them said something about how she and her ex had gotten a divorce, but after a period they got back together. Her comment was something like, "Men are Stuck on Stupid or 'SOS'," as she put it. I had to laugh at her, but I guess she meant that when one person in a marriage seems to do something stupid, the other person must deal with their actions.

The best example I saw regarding, "Stuck on Stupid" that night was another guy whom I met in this group. These words, or something like them, were his motto too. His wife had died from cancer over six years ago, and he was still referring to her as "his wife." It was as if she was still alive and somehow, she would be back one day. I guess he had never gotten over her death, and the whole night he never let a sentence go by without mentioning her. It was very uncomfortable to sit near him and hear almost every word that came out of his mouth referred to her. Don't get me wrong, I really did feel for him and his loss. However, his life must really be stuck in Park since he cannot move forward with any new relationship. In every other way, he seemed as if he had it together, but he had acted as if he had his one chance to meet his "soul mate," and now he wasn't allowed to have another for the rest of his life—how sad?

Will this be the sob story for every person who can't move forward with his or her life? What part of "move on" don't they get? Do they feel that comfortable, or uncomfortable in this case, that they will flounder in sorrow until they die? Besides, do they want every new person they meet to feel their pain? After talking with this guy for only a few minutes, I wanted to crawl into a hole just to get away from him. Even though he was a very attractive and distinguished guy, I had a hard time getting by the "wife" comments all night long. He's got to deal with that "time" of his life to make sure the garbage disposal isn't stuck regurgitating the same stink.

I just wonder how he even deals with all the other issues in life since he can't deal with her death. Was it his age that made a difference? He really wasn't that old, just in his late 50s, but I don't know if that had anything to do with the whole situation. Isn't death supposed to be an ending to something that was once a beginning, and we should remember the good times more than the bad? Besides, who said that one shouldn't move on and find true love again and be should be stuck with an arrow to their heart for eternity. I mean I'm dealing with so many changes still, that people around me are amazed that I'm still breathing air into my lungs.

My newest challenge is selling this home that I don't want to be living in. I now know why I hate selling a home—all the cleaning, straightening up and cancelled showings take a toll on you. Out of the 10 house showings, that were supposed to happen, I think only seven have showed up. With the economy being the way it is, everyone thinks they can get something for nothing. I guess I'm in that category too, because I did find a townhouse at an awesome price. I didn't even have to argue about the cost, I just took it. For, I knew that I couldn't get anything else brand new and at that price. Now, if I can only get off the Deed of Trust on this house to rid my commitment to this property.

My ex is playing hardball once again, and now doesn't want to pay for child support and is using this against me. If I let him out of child support, he'll take over the current residence. Isn't that black mail? I guess I should have consulted with a lawyer about this house during the divorce. But I was trying to save money, and handling the house situation is one thing not on our divorce decree. We had verbally agreed that my son and I would stay here as long as I wanted. Little did I know, those horrid memories never went away, and now I'm stuck trying to get all the pieces of my life back into an order that once again makes sense.

All the paint, the new furniture, and the new pictures didn't convince my psyche that this home is mine and only mine. However, this must be resolved this week, so my loan will go through smoothly. Besides, if he tries to play hardball, I'm using my wits to counteract his attitude. I'm sure he's getting advice from his "Chickypoo" since she knows all about divorce, and how to cheat on your spouse. You know, the one he chose to cheat on me with—his two-time cheater/loser?

It seems the more things he throws my way; I keep coming up with something else to throw back. I think he thought that I would just bow down and still try to please him—once again. Well, guess what, he obviously doesn't know me that well! After 19 years of being with him, this divorce has taught me to stand up for myself, and not let him get over anything on me—ever again.

Divorce sometimes will break a person, but I think my background of being the youngest child, a female, and a military veteran, has taught me to speak up. Believe me, I wasn't always this way. I was once shy, backward, and I let people tell me what to do—just like a robot. My self-esteem was low, and I never really knew how to take up for myself. I think it was when I went into the military that I finally blossomed into someone who took charge and didn't let the bastards get me down. It took a few years, but it was a learned behavior, I think, that finally gave me the confidence to succeed. The more responsibility I was given, the more I had to organize my thoughts to take care of everything. This was a lesson I needed, and it served me well.

Speaking of lessons learned, I look back now to this Sunday's service. The Pastor said something that referred to making decisions in one's life. He said that you must have peace within yourself when making major decisions. There must also be an open door and a desire to make your decision. Lastly, you must feel calm about the situation. These words were so true this past week. The first townhouse that I had made an offer on was a little more than I wanted to spend, so I didn't offer any more than I could afford. However, the second one was less money and brand-new. Talk about timing!

That "peace" he described is well within me this time, and I know this is the right choice. I'm still scared of my moves since this is one more decision that I'm making on my own, but it's a necessary one. For, I think my ex believes he can still control my every move. As I said before, when he wanted me to do something for him, he expected it to be done right away. If I wanted him to do something for me, it was on his own time frame, and I had to constantly ask him to do it. I never realized how that had affected me until now, and how much energy it took. He constantly controlled my moves, and I just let him take that control to the max. Now that I'm not allowing his controlling ways to affect me, as before, he's mad that he cannot take charge of any situation in which we're both involved. I guess once a control freak, always a control freak, right? But, think of it this way, God does direct you in the route to which you're most effective. Just asking for guidance is the first step.

I think I've finally found my calling, and I have finally taken back control in my life that once was lost. Since my ex and I have parted ways, I look back now, and it still amazes me how a relationship between two people becomes a whole. Then if the situation warrants something new down the road, each person can go off in two different directions. Sometimes you can get back together, but other times a marriage can end up in divorce. Two people with two different personalities originally meshed into one entity are now null and void.

Sometimes marriage works, but other times—like my situation—it becomes a condition where one personality becomes domineering and the other becomes submissive. I guess I don't get it when one person feels they must take control of their significant other or someone will take their "control" away from them. How scary is that? Besides, each day that I go towards a different pursuit, I seem to be presented with different challenges. My friends who are going through a divorce or have been through a divorce, in addition to myself, have dealt with it differently. Some days we are upbeat and giddy as compared to other days that really get us down.

My friend, Jackie, has been on a roll lately. She seems to be having so much fun being single and finally getting out of there dating new guys and hanging out with friends. You know—real life as compared to her train wreck of a marriage oh so long ago? Well, she told me today that she cried herself to sleep last night. What the heck happened? Personally, I think that she's having flash backs of her marriage, or where she's going next—it has been two years since she was divorced. Maybe I'm wrong. She did, however, meet a new guy over the weekend and just had lunch with him yesterday. He thanked her for meeting him for lunch. Hello? Did she meet a guy who was nice to her? She's told me for months now that she's not looking for a relationship. But that's usually when you meet someone—when you're not looking, right! I had always been told that, but never really believed it, but I guess it could be true.

As for me, my relationship with the guy I met in late September still exists—for now anyway. He has some personal issues from his past relationships, and he is also currently dealing with some family concerns. He tells me that he will try to sell his condo, again, by the end of the year and then move. I asked him where he would move to, and his response was, "Perhaps, I'll end up at your doorstep." Well, I'm not giving it too much thought, because he's run the other direction before—at least three times. I just know in my heart that he wants to be with me, but he has had to deal with his own issues before he can really and truly be involved with me. So, I'm doing my own thing and not placing much emphasis on us being together—permanently, anyway. I'm taking care of my son and me right now, and if something good comes about, far be it for me to complain. Our relationship seems to be a broken record, and it keeps repeating itself constantly. I don't know about you, but it sounds like the lyrics don't need to be repeated.

With all of the emotions tied to divorce, supporting your children on a limited budget always seems to be at the top of that list. I constantly see women whose husbands either left them with the shirt on their backs, pay them very little each month, or step up to the plate to take care of their kids. They seem to struggle constantly with their ex and deal with their kids on a full-time basis because they are the sole support.

As for my ex and I, we have our days when we wish we had never laid eyes on each other. Other days, we talk like we've never had a care in the world in the two decades we've known each other. Lately, we've made some decisions to completely delete the ties that bind us—like the home we had together. I'm moving on to a new home; he's at his new place, and the home we bought together will hopefully be sold—and soon. We both agree that we hate that place. There seem to be too many bad memories for both of us, and selling the house is the only way to dispose of those dreadful feelings. We both must move on to get past those emotions we felt in that structure. The constant struggles, and the mean voices we both heard over the cries of our son trying to stop our words, have left us both tragically suffering inside.

I know I want to grow into a person who is happier than the one I will leave in this current home. I didn't like who I had become in this place. The hurtful phrases we both used made us very unhappy and unworthy of each other. Hopefully, now we can grow into that person we always hoped we could become. Maybe this house needs a "cleansing" or a voodoo spell to obliterate the bad vibes it gives off. I just hope the next family who lives here has better luck than us.

7th Chapter

Dismount!

Moving ahead and not looking behind you, I guess, is a learned trait that we all must do when we are hurting. For example, a co-worker the other day said something to me that really hit home. She said, "The horse is dead. It's time to dismount!" It's as if she could read my mind when it came to divorce. She should know because she was married three times before the right guy came into her life. Her third marriage did the trick; she's been married over 27 years now, and happy as can be. She admits the first two marriages shouldn't have happened, but she never gave up the fight.

It's also interesting to me how things in life redirect you to where you should have been in the first place. I guess it's the decisions we make after we realize that our current situation should go away since it could really make our life better. Adjusting to that idea is hard and difficult situations seem to come our way for a very long time after divorce. It's only after the right person comes along, to sweep you off your feet, does your life change—and hopefully for the better. When we finally meet this person, I guess you both can look back and realize one thing. If you had met long before you were married to that "wrong" person, your life would have gone in a totally different direction. But would you really be able to see life as you do now? Would life's lessons, up until this point, have taught you everything you needed to know to survive to this very moment? It's a crapshoot, I guess because we can never go back on those "what ifs."

Life has so many questions and issues to deal with each day, so we have to be on our toes. Concerns seem to raise their ugly little heads, and how one deals with it says something about one's character. The people I've met this past year since my divorce have shown me how they deal with their lives since their significant other left. For example, I've noticed that the men I've met seem to deal with multi-tasking in a whole other way than women. Men who have a lot to deal with on their plate seem to "freak out" or I guess, just "lose it" when it comes to things that affect them personally.

The age of the man also seems to have some significance; especially, if they've been on their own for a very long time. On the other hand, the women I've known seem to deal with tragedies and loss better than men. A few men I've known seem to run away and not let anyone else in their lives, nor do they talk about their ex which still affects their heart and their future relationships. They can't get past those ancient times and learn to grow into a new relationship.

It seems like they are so comfortable in those old shoes of theirs, a new pair may not fit, or "it" will turn into a blister—if you know what I mean! Perhaps a wound would form and rub them the wrong way, which will remind them that something new is not always good. This way of thinking is so narrow-minded, at least in my book. They feel that they will never be able to let go and find the "one" they were meant for—perhaps for the first time in a very long time.

I once knew a guy who was so stuck on a lady from his past, he couldn't move forward. We, at first, were just friends, and then he started feeling something for me. Unfortunately, I just wanted him as a friend and besides, I knew this past relationship would have always been at the back of his mind. I didn't want to be "second best" with him, nor do I ever want that with anyone. I truly believe that a relationship should be a shared one in which each person truly values the other. Another guy I dated in the 80s was so infatuated with "us" and was starting to make plans with me in his future. He was a nice guy, but my feelings weren't the same. I couldn't lead him on, so I ended it. To this day, I hope that he did find that special someone; I just know it wasn't me. There goes that "crap shoot" again, huh?

Today in church the topic was "Reflections on Marriage." It's a little ironic that in just two months, the anniversary when I "busted" my ex will happen. It was Father's Day, June 22, 2009, that changed my life forever. This morning's sermon made me really think about how my life was then, as compared to now. One of the things mentioned was to forget the past and focus on today. I guess marriage problems can start from the sins of one or both people straying from the words they once said to each other.

Selfishness and separation in a relationship is like a train going down the wrong tracks; only to hit a brick wall at the end of the line. When the words of one or both people mean nothing anymore, or when one person "falls out of love" with the other, doomsday is bound to happen. The marriage has died and the only thing that can happen now is a parting of the ways. One or both people seem to look away from the other, and they can't bear to touch, nor can they look at each other in the eye, for their love has fallen from grace.

A healthy marriage should consist of wanting to be with the other, touching and holding one another and never wanting to let go. You long for that person and never feel as complete in yourself as you once were when you were single. You miss each other when you're apart, and you long for the next time you see them. It sounds too good to be true for me to be at this point again. But I need that emotional completeness!

I guess it still surprises me that people can fall out of love just as easily as they fall in love. What goes wrong in a marriage can consist of little things or they can be gigantic. But the way we deal with a problem is what gets us to the next level. Is it worth it to stay in a relationship, just to be a family unit, for the kids, finances, or some other reason? I guess some people really think things will change or get better, but for the most part, if a relationship is bound to break apart, it will. Plus, if we do nothing, how will anything change for the better? Is adopting social norms a reason to stay together? Just because our parents stayed together for the wrong reasons, should we do the same if we are totally miserable? Probably not!

My neighbor had that idea—once—but she's finally gotten to the point of no return. She's finally realized that things are not going to change in the relationship with her significant other, and she must create a new life. She must start a venue without him, so that her two sons will not commit the same sins for which she is running away from. She must set an example for them to emulate. Her strength is what will keep her on the right track—I just know it. She, along with many others, must do what is right for herself and for her children. Besides, our mothers put up with too much crap in their time—we shouldn't have to commit the same sin today because we are stronger now in so many ways, right?

So, is the grass truly greener on the other side of the fence when it comes to a significant other? When that important person tiptoes over to the greener pastures, it seems their first thoughts tell them how great it would be to stay there. Has their heart been hardened so badly towards us that they can't see beyond the forest for there are now too many trees in their way? When they lose that loving feeling for you, do they compare it to Christ losing the feeling he had for you when he was on the cross? I don't think so.

So, what are the reasons to get married? Well, according to the Pastor this morning they are: 1) children, 2) intimacy, 3) a completion to remove loneliness in your life, and 4) to mirror and model yourself for all to see in Christ's church. Now, if these are the reasons to get married, what are the reasons to get divorced? How do you fall out of love, after a certain time, with that special person that you once loved with all your heart? Why do you never want to see that person who now despises you, or vice versa? Does anyone ever want to get to this point; I think not. Does anyone want to hurt as badly as they do when that special person tosses them to their side? Again, the answer is no. I think people should love themselves as much as they do their spouse. Because love equals respect, right? Well, it should! If we all felt as confident with ourselves as we do with that special person, life would be good, or would it? I wish I had the answers to life's little questions. For if I did would I'd be the popular one? Then, I'd have another set of problems to deal with, I guess?

So, how do we not destroy our original feelings for our soul mate? Can we remember to respect one another and constantly show the "one" how much we care for them on a consistent basis? We should repeat this pattern as often as possible. Remember those first acts of kindness and feelings of completeness that were present when we first met them? We never took advantage of that special one, it wasn't even a thought in our brain. We should remember why we first wanted that person in our lives, and why we constantly had good thoughts about him or her. Ok, here we go with that thought that love equals respect again. This should work on a two-way basis, right? So, to have a relationship, I think both people should be on the same page. They should both be able to trust each other—always. So, who does this work out for? Perhaps it could be Cinderella? Well, she shouldn't have all the luck.

In divorce as well as life, which continually changes, one's mind can race and totally mess up your sleeping patterns. It was for me since last night I was constantly tossing and turning. I kept waking up because so many things in my life are changing—still. I am proceeding towards being the new owner of a townhouse. This entails looking for the right place, the loan application, and catching every curve ball that is set towards my site. So far, I have managed to get all the information the loan officer needs and somehow the townhouse got lost in this mess. I wanted a fireplace, but it was missing in the original contract. I'm sure I could get out of this contract, but I like the location and since it's new, I would be the first owner. Besides, the view is awesome, and I could always add a fireplace later.

I guess things happen for a reason—or at least that's what I keep getting told. It was very liberating today. I signed over my current home to my ex and now I'm free of this monstrosity for good. I can only look forward to my next home—mine. We even have an offer on this house, and tomorrow there's a second showing at this house. Strange, isn't it? When you don't care if something happens, it does. I guess it's like the relationship I have with this guy I've been seeing on and off. Tonight, I was with him, and it's as if I have turned off my feelings for him. It felt strange. Since he must get his life in order before we could "really" be together, I have put my feelings on the shelf for now. I talk to him daily, but I cannot let him get too close because I know he will run away again. Staying at arm's length is what I need to do now.

For once, I feel like I'm in control of my future. I am going ahead with my needs, and not letting any male in my life determine my moves. I know I cannot be with anyone on a permanent basis; at least for now. I even raised my hand in church yesterday when the Pastor was talking about marriage, and he wanted to know who had no desire to get married. Boy, that was a surprise to me. I guess my attitude has changed in the past few weeks. My strength has grown from a sapling to a full-fledged tree spreading its branches outward creating shade for that newly grown grass under my feet. It feels like I've finally taken control over my fate. Although I've thought about this before, it's now different. Now, I'm going to be in "my" home and not "his" home. I feel a new air about myself. I know I can accomplish this new project; I just need positive thoughts.

I think my mind is overloaded. Between putting an offer on a townhouse, keeping my current home clean for showings since it's on the market, getting my loan paperwork together, and getting insurance on the new place, I think I may lose my mind. I'm still a single mom with a son living with me every other week. I'm also packing a little each night to get ready for my move in five weeks. No wonder I can't sleep very well. I even had a co-worker tell me yesterday that once everything settles down, then and only then, I will be bored. Imagine that! Me, bored? This last year has been so hectic and life changing; I have gone from married with a son to a divorced white female with child (a.k.a. DWFWC).

The relationships I've had have also changed me. I've only gone out with two guys since my divorce almost a year ago, and both still make me wonder why I still need a man. I even had a dream last night about the one guy I still see. In the dream, he bought the townhouse beside me. Now, why would I go there? I don't understand some of the dreams I have had in the past several months. Do I have some unseated feelings that I still need to deal with? Do I somehow wish that my life would settle down and I would meet a guy who will sweep me off my feet? But why would I go there right now? Am I really ready for a new relationship? Just a few days ago I decided that I'm going on with my life and I'm not letting any man determine my future. I must depend on me—and only me—to survive. With the help of God to help me get to the next step of my life, I'll make it. When I was hoping that this relationship would complete me, I was really stressed. Now, I'm not feeling that emotion. I feel much better since I know I can make it by myself. It feels weird that I can have those emotions, but they are welcomed.

Life is starting to feel a little strange today since I've been packing, I showed my friend my townhouse, and sold my dining table to another friend. It's now 9 p.m., and I am standing in the dining room looking around at this house, which was once a home, but now it's just a dwelling that I will be in for another 25 days and then I will leave forever. Today is May 1, 2010, and the calendar says I have just over three weeks before I will have my own place. Yes, my own home, without my ex. One which he did not approve of, nor did he help me finance. I got this on my own—no man in my life had anything to do with my decision. I have made it to this point in my life, and I am proud of myself. What a powerful force I now have in my life—ME! Scary huh?

As the packing continues, the closets are now becoming empty, the pictures on the wall are leaving an empty space and the boxes are piling up in the dining room as well as in the garage. I even threw away that wreath that my ex-sister-in-law made for us when we moved into our last home. It was a huge arrangement with twigs, fake fruit, and even a pheasant pelt. It was a beautiful arrangement—she really was good at her passion. Before we moved into this home, I painstakingly cleaned every twig, and every piece attached to the base of the arrangement. But, this time, the dust had overtaken every part of it, and I decided not to keep it. I was so pleased with myself when I opened the trash can lid and threw that "thing" away. I want new memories, and not ones I had with him.

I also wonder about my ex sometimes. Was he completely happy with his decision to leave us? Does he really know where his life will end up and is this girlfriend just using him to "fix" up her home? Will she let him go after she gets what she wants? At this point in the game, I really don't care, because I'm finally moving forward without them both. It's so nice not to have to ask his permission for anything. I just told him I was moving and signed the house back to him. It was easier than I thought it would be.

Well, it happened, May 1 has arrived, and in exactly 25 days I will be the owner of a new town home. I woke up today, and thought to myself, "Oh Crap, I have 25 days. I'd better get packing—literally!"

Now, here's another episode of the saga that made me really think that I'm really moving ahead of this battle. You know that one occurrence that changed your life and every little thing afterwards is such a struggle? I guess they make various brands of wine for these little issues in life, huh? Also, today I bought a garage door opener for my new place and scheduled the installation for the afternoon that I close. Besides this, I also scheduled the cable guy to come and install Internet and cable in the two bedrooms upstairs. Boy, I feel that I'm spending money like its water coming out of my spigot. But I'm getting what I need accomplished. Plus, I also feel that I'm getting deeper into debt. I think another glass of wine is in order—don't you think? Don't get me wrong, I'm not turning into an alcoholic, I guess I just sometimes need to relax and enjoy life, and a glass of wine does that for me. I had an alcoholic dad, so I know when enough is enough.

This new adventure in my life will be good for me, I just know it. Organization is now my key to getting what I want out of life. Today, I even called an ex-neighbor to get in touch with a friend so I can schedule some light fixtures to be installed. He has his own electrical business; plus, I know him, so I can trust him to get the job done right. So, now I have three people coming in the afternoon of closing. I figure that I can close that morning, and then move a few things myself before everyone comes at 1pm. Then, the next day, I can have the movers come and take everything from the house, I'm currently in, and move everything to the new place. I pride myself on getting things moving at a constant pace, so I hope this goes smoothly. I don't like a lot of chaos but guess what I'm prepared for if it happens.

So, how does life go on when chaos is the name of the game? I may be the perfect poster child for that subject. I have had so much happen in my life right now, I'm surprised I remember to still breathe. I guess the key is to organize like you've never organized before. This week I've also checked the progress of my new place and additionally arranged the cable, electricity, gas, and water to be turned on. The cable guy, garage door guy, and an ex-neighbor should arrive in the afternoon. Wow! I must pinch myself to know that I'm still among the humans still alive in the world.

I'm totally exhausted from packing, cleaning, and trying to fit in a workout at night, in addition to going to physical therapy at noon twice a week. I'm lucky to remember my name and to turn on the alarm clock before I go to sleep. Where would I be without organization? I am writing everything down, so I won't forget, and grabbing a piece of paper and a pencil when I think of the next thing to accomplish or schedule. I guess dating is the last thing on my list right now, but it's still a priority. So, how do I proceed?

The one thing that I have noticed about dating again is the fact they we get stuck in a rut from being alone for so long, or we can't stand to be alone at all. What makes us so stubborn in our ways that we cannot conform to a "norm?" I guess it's a little different now that we're in our 40s and 50s, for we now know what we want in life? Or do we? We try to fit another person in our existence, but sometimes we're not willing to change our routine to accommodate them. So, why do we even try? Are we such a culture that we must have a significant other in our life and then make them accommodate our life? Whatever the case, dating is so complicated—more so than in our teens. I guess it takes kissing a lot of frogs (for both with men and women) to find "the one" for each of us. We also must know where we want to be in life or we will never get there—well, at least that's my thought.

I don't think we really know where we want to be, but a plan helps. So, now your homework is to write a plan. Get a pencil and paper and write where you want to be in six months, one year, and five years. Sounds a little intimidating, huh? If you think of it as a step-by-step process and take it a small piece at a time, you can make it happen. For me, it started by packing up as much of my ex's belongings as possible, painting the walls, getting new furniture, buying a new truck, and then making the decision to buy my own place. I know this is a lot to digest, but I sometimes make decisions quicker than some people. But I always believed that I shouldn't let any grass grow under my feet, and to go for something that really makes me happy. It's something that's taken a lot of energy and time out of my life. I didn't say it was easy, for I've felt literally sick on occasions just because I thought I was making another mistake in my life. So, is treading lightly the game plan unless you have a cast-iron stomach? I guess we just must think about it for a few minutes, hours, days, etc.

Other divorced people that I've seen sometimes let their friends make their life decisions for them. Peer pressure weighs heavily on their shoulders even though they're older now. In addition, culture has dictated their fate, and they are powerless to do anything because it would be "wrong" in everyone's eyes. What? Who made those rules? Are we not adults? Do we not pay our own bills and go to work without someone holding our hand? I guess some people need a little push to "grow up" once again. Hopefully, they will listen to those words of wisdom from their friends and family, and it will sink in—at least one day.

So, how do you convince someone that they should pursue what they want, vice do what their friends and family say they should do? Especially, when someone is in their 50s and they are trying to conform to their surroundings. How do you convince someone that they've hit "adult" status, and that they shouldn't have to obey the rules of others? My option is that you should take everything into account; you know, inhale it, digest it, but then make your own decision. Gee, that makes too much sense, huh? This is the case with the guys I've met this last year. They have their own agenda, their own ways of doing things, and they seem to be stuck in a rut in one form or another.

It's not just men or just women who have fallen into this trap of Divorced White Male/Female. It seems that everyone deals with divorce in their own way, but it's never easy, and never the same. For example, today I had an appointment with my doctor who is going through a divorce. His wife had a habit of going down that path of self-destruction when they were together. She would always make excuses for not getting a job, so she went to school for years. Then, he found out that she was having an affair. He's now moved out and gotten a roommate, and the "soon to be ex" wants whatever money and support she feels she deserves. But one evening he made a decision that changed his future; he couldn't make himself go home and stay in the same dwelling they have together.

So, he asked a friend to let him spend the night, and he never went back to his wife. He just moved his things out when she wasn't home.

So, will women ever understand men? Or vice versa? We are such different creatures that it's surprising we can even exist on the planet together. I even wonder about the guy I've known now for eight months. He is so close to me, but still so far away. He won't allow me to truly understand him. He doesn't want to grow old alone, but he won't let anyone, especially me, get anywhere near his emotions, his family, or his friends. It seems he only wants me for one thing. Is this really what I want in my life now? At this point, I really don't know. Intimacy is important, but at what cost to my psyche. However, I know I want someone to share their inner most thoughts, but where do you find a man who will let their guard down?

From what I've seen this past year, I keep finding out more things about men and divorce. Men seem to take their feelings and hide them in a box and then try to prove their manhood. Women, I've found, seem to cry until the tears have run out. The time that passes between relationships, and I mean real relationships, is quite critical. If all you want to do is satisfy your sexual feelings, and not deal with your true emotions, you'll never really understand how to deal with the right person who comes into your life.

The damage can be permanently engulfed in a person's life, and if it isn't resolved it won't go away. There's a lot of harm that's done to one's heart when divorce occurs; especially if one cheats on their spouse. The bleeding seems to occur inside your soul, and it never really stops. It may be plugged up with bitterness and one-night stands, but it never really heals. All of that hatred, war wounds and pain still exist, and it can be inside of you for years. A person must really look at it through their eyes and personally confront it. In my case, I just wrote about my fears, my hatred, and my loneliness.

Currently, I have a man in my life who has done nothing but pursue women to heal his bodily functions, and nothing else. So, why do I stay in his life? There's just something about him that intrigues me, but it may not be enough for us to make it to eternity. He runs away as fast as he can get his shoes on his feet. He won't let me near him as close as I'd like; he keeps me at an arm's length so that I won't get too close to him. Is he afraid that if he lets me in, I will hurt him as much as his past relationships? I really think this is true. I guess he hasn't had much reason to trust in a true relationship, and I confuse his emotions. I really believe that he's not sure what to think of me. I am blunt, honest, and overly compassionate towards him, and it seems he is not used to someone who is so different than the others he's dated. Maybe I wanted to be a counselor at one time in my life; I guess that's where I get that part of me who is willing to go the extra mile to succeed in getting him out of his shell.

So, what makes a person retreat into a shell when a new relationship comes from nowhere? Why would a person who is looking to be fulfilled not jump on something they know will be good for them? On the other hand, why does a person willingly give their heart to someone whom they know is not right for them? Should we just "settle" for a person just because we're lonely or because it's our time to just get married according to our parents? Does peer pressure, all around us, dictate our decisions before and during our marriage, then after our divorce? Even though we want something that others around us think we shouldn't have, do we go with what they advise, versus our own wants and needs? I guess the question should be, "When do we finally stand up for what we want out of life?" When do we exercise our rights, our values, and our desires against our religious beliefs and our friends? Is there a time when we finally put our foot down and say, "This is what I want out of life, and damn it, I deserve it!"

Even though our upbringing has taught us values and how we regard others and our God, how do we put it in perspective for our own life? Is a certain religion not what we want? Do we see, and read, between the lines and not what does happen? Plus, is our religion commanding too much of us? Is our life so surrounded with so many rules and regulations that we wonder why we chose a certain religion at all? Or it could be just the opposite; we could have no religion at all in our lives, which is leading us down the path of destruction. Either way we live, we must have a balance somehow. Plus, don't we need directions for our life? We must choose a path that will get us to the goal we set for our future.

Getting to where we need to be may come from a person you least expect. Just when I thought I had taught everything I know to my little sister, she surprised me today. She said that her life got better after her divorce because she finally started taking care of herself—for once. At one time, she was taking care of her invalid father and her husband. I guess sometimes we get stuck in such a rut that we don't realize that we have become someone else whom we don't even recognize anymore.

As a wife and mother, I gave my all to my husband and son. Everything they needed from me, I provided or attempted to provide. Somewhere, I lost track because I should have taken care of me too. My weight went up, and my every action was to serve them and their every whim. I guess I finally realized what was happening when my ex had an affair; it was only then I realized that everything that I had done for him was ignored and not appreciated. Finally, I understood that it was my turn to become the person that I wanted and needed to be, since it was me who had been taken advantage of for years. I didn't count for some reason, and I allowed it to occur for a very long time. I guess it just didn't happen overnight, it was a very slow, steady process. How did I let myself get to that low point of my life? I didn't take the time to take care of my diet, my health, and myself in general. Ouch!

I've seen dominance brought on by men before—for it happened in my family. When I was growing up, I saw my family get together around the dining room table at my grandmother's house when it was harvesting season (i.e. butchering, bringing in hay for the winter, etc.). First the men were seated, and only when they were done eating, the women sat down for their meal. When they sat down, the food was cold, and so was the atmosphere. I saw this when I was in elementary school, and I hated this tradition. The explanation was that the men were working outside, and they basically "deserved" to be fed first because they needed to get back to work. Hello? Who did the preparation for the meal, and worked inside for the whole day? All of this makes sense now, because I was "taught" to take care of a man who expected the same treatment, and I allowed it to happen. Why? I guess we do what we know, and we marry what is comfortable. Scary, huh?

I sometimes hate myself for allowing myself to take care of my family the way I did. I guess it's how an addict thinks. Being comfortable and feeling content with situations as a child is what makes us do a lot of what we do as adults. Our childhood has sculpted our thoughts and ideals and as we get older, sometimes we fall back on what we know—even though we don't agree with it. What we know sometimes can be our downfall, especially in marriage. When we retreat, we are scared and run away from an issue that needs to be fixed, and often that issue remains unchecked. Then, we involve another individual, who gets caught up in our trap, and ends up getting hurt. Can we allow this to happen? I don't believe we see it happening until the hurt and pain of divorce enter our lives. Then, guess what? We don't have the control we thought we once had, and running back to our "norm" is our only answer.

Well, today I hit another milestone. It's Mother's Day, and here I am sitting at my kitchen table reviewing my life once again. One more month will mark the anniversary when I confronted "him." The house seems so quiet today. Even though my son is upstairs talking on the phone to his grandma, all I hear is the rumble of the dryer. I'm not sure how to think or even what to think. Mary even texted me last evening to let me know of her depression. Her ex had given her a card last year on this day to say what a loving and caring wife he had. Then one month later all Hell broke loose and her life was changed forever. I guess some of my pain is still there, but I have moved forward quicker than my friends and family realize. I have broken out of the cocoon and now a beautiful butterfly has emerged—flying freely.

Even though I'm still struggling with issues in my life, I have come to the realization that I was never meant to be with my ex. His controlling ways and the tension that I felt when I was around him were more than I could bear. But I never realized how much his actions affected me until I knew he was unfaithful. I sometimes wonder why he did what he did, but I know his decisions will come to haunt him eventually. I truly believe in karma! As for me, I am still trying to resolve the "moving" process in my life. I just found out yesterday that my closing date has been postponed for one day and that my walk-through day has been delayed for a week. Now, I must make all those phone calls again to the agencies that will provide my water, electricity, and gas. In addition, there are more calls to those individuals who were supposed to show up on the afternoon of closing. This was one more thing that kept me up last night. The stress has not left my side, but I think it is good stress—if you can call it that. At least I don't have to worry about someone coming home and yelling at me about nothing. The only individual in my life that does that at my home is my cat—and I can't understand his words—just his tone and actions.

Today, Mother's Day, I went to church and found myself with tears in my eyes for the first 30 minutes. A baby was baptized and the most significant thing about him was that he had fallen from a three-story window a few weeks back and he survived. They showed a video, which showed him in the hospital recovering from his injuries. I don't know what lead to him to fall, but I know that when I saw his parents up on stage, they seemed forever grateful that their son had made a full recovery—today, I saw a "complete" family, unlike my own.

I know it's the norm to first get married then to have children. But how proper is it to get married, have children, and then get a divorce? The children are still in the picture, but the marriage is in a faraway place that no one can see or feel. The only thing left is the hurt feelings, the memories of good and bad, and the day-to-day activities that must still occur. Each person lives a new life far removed from his or her prior life as a couple, and now each holiday, event, or school play is somehow different.

Mother's Day is almost gone and there is a little of me that is left of the emotions of prior years. I don't know what to think about today. Will I feel the same about Father's Day next month? Because it was that weekend that my ex was busted and then he moved out. This first year has been very hard for me because everything is different—even though the divorce papers have a very thin layer of dust on them. Just because I am "free," doesn't mean that I truly am free. Life is still going on around me, and it's happening without my permission. I can no longer control the events around me; I can only control my actions and my words. I must try to live my life, as I would want my son to live when he becomes an adult.

This evening, I am still thinking about today's events. The church service, the packing, and my new "relationship" that totally engulfs me since it began eight months ago. It seems that every major holiday he runs in the other direction. Today was no exception. He found another excuse to let me go once again; I'm sure my text message made him think. It said, "Once again—another holiday, another goodbye." Later I sent him another one that said, "Each time you say goodbye, I get a piece of my heart back that you once took.

Soon, I'll be healed completely, I hope, and I won't feel hurt anymore so I can completely go on alone—yeah, right! Can he say the same?" I must have hit a nerve because my nose started itching several times after that one. Maybe I don't truly understand him, but a friend told me last week that if he won't talk to you now, why would he talk to you if you married him? She's got a point, and why would I put myself in a situation where I want someone like that? I mean, he's 58 years old. Is he going to grow up any time soon? Is any guy I meet going to be mature enough to let go of their hurt, deal with their current life, and then move on? At this point in my life, I'm not sure. But I truly feel more freedom since I have decided to let him go because I'm not worrying about how we will be when we're together. Once I decided not to worry about us being together, that feeling of independence came back to me once more. I am not dealing with his ideals of coping with what his friends and family will think of me because I'm white and he's Latino.

In my family, my dad was very vocal about other races, and watching that in my life and in his, made me change my attitude as a child and I have kept that desire in my adulthood. I have dated men who were of mixed race, and I accepted that fact. The only thing I haven't liked, about any of these men, was their attitude. It didn't matter what they looked like outside, it was how they treated me that counted. I have found that "a man is a man is a man", and lately I'm finding that they all have that "male" gene that is very unyielding. They're all stuck in a rut from not dealing with their past lives, and they continue in their current life and don't make room for me. I can't deal with someone who doesn't want to fit me in their lives, you know, make room for me, as I would them? Have they all gotten so comfortable with their skin that changing their lifestyle would hinder their being? I don't have the answers; I just wish I could figure out men!

The world keeps spinning around without my permission, just as the people around me keep making decisions about their own fate. Do they still want me in their life? Are they as sick of my past relationships as I am? I remember when a friend of mine went through a divorce years ago; she so seemed miserable for such a long time. It was as if I was her sounding board, and after several months of hearing her fate, I was numb with her pain. I wasn't sure I really wanted to hear any more about what happened with her relationship.

I wanted to be there for her, but on the other hand, I wanted to put my head in the sand to not listen to her troubles. I felt sad for her and wanted to be her shoulder to cry on, but it seemed that PTSD set in and the more I heard her words, the more it started to affect me. I guess I'm now at that point in my life where I can't spill my guts as it has almost been one year since my life changed. Even this evening there was another gut-wrenching blow. My son and I had dinner together and he mentioned that his dad and the girlfriend were looking at BMWs and planning a cruise to the Bahamas. I wasn't sure if I wanted to be angry, upset, or cry. He never wanted to do anything fun when we were together, nor did he ever want to go on a cruise ship, especially with me. He didn't believe in something like that!

So, when will their "honeymoon" cease? Are they so happy together now that they've "proven" they can be in a state of euphoria forever? He never wanted to be in a relationship like that with me. Somehow, I still feel a little inadequate, but if I look at my life now, I'm gaining some ground too. I just know it's not his money they're spending for that perfect life. He's really sucking air for an income because his business is really getting so difficult now. So, when will she wake up and realize he's just a big phony when he says one day he'll be rich. He tried to become rich when we were together, for almost two decades, and he couldn't make it—he failed! Gee, are we now in a competition? Are we both trying to see who can become like the "Jones's"? I think since he's with her, the road to becoming rich is shortening. At least I'm realistic in knowing that I need to be on my own instead of running to the next person who has money and will pick my clothes off the floor when I when I put on my PJ's. I really think he "has" to have a person in his life.

At this point in time, I don't have to have a man. Although, I would like to share my hopes and dreams with someone, but I will not settle for just anyone—not this time! God, just give me a direction, please! Can you say, "Dismount?"

8th Chapter

Three, two, one…launch?

I think I have the arrows to my next direction. My loan just got approved, and my townhouse is almost completed. I checked on it last night and the cabinets are in, the hardwood floors are down, and they were beginning to paint the doors. This weekend the tile goes up in the bathrooms and in the kitchen. Wow! I am so mentally and physically exhausted I can't think anymore. I still have packing to do, but for the last three nights I've either had errands to do, or last night I just came home, got on the treadmill and then collapsed in bed. This brings back so many memories of when my ex and I originally bought this house and were moving from our old home. It was me who packed everything for the move, took care of our son, and held a full-time job. This time I'm not packing "his" stuff, but what I find that belongs to him will be put it in the basement. Once again, I have had to pick up the pieces of my life with him in it—STILL! Well, guess what? This time it's all about my son and me. I've concluded that the things I don't want in this house are staying here. If he doesn't want it, it will be here for the new owners. Besides, next weekend is my garage sale; time to get rid of the things we once had together. This will be such a fresh start for me to get rid of those "things" that hold such bad memories. I'm looking forward to disposing of those items and buying something new for me. It's an exciting time, but also highly stressful. Will my life ever settle down? I certainly hope so, but then I'll complain I'm bored. I guess this "divorce" thing never really goes away; it just changes. But remember, if you want your life to change, you can't sleepwalk through the process; wake up and find those arrows that point your way!

So, think of divorce like this, each time I go out with friends, I realize that I am not the only one who was "hit" with this new life. One of the guys in our singles group last night made me realize that we all have something in common. Each one of us has been divorced, but struggling really wasn't in any of our vocabularies. His ex-wife served him with divorce papers on the same day he took his daughter to college. His response to the whole thing was more of a concern for his daughter than for him, due to the shock it had to her system. Like him, my concern was for my son who had been on a vacation with his grandmother. He was shocked when he came home and was presented with our news. The confusion to him must have been not of this world.

I think children know what is going on; we should at least give them that much credit. They have an idea that things aren't right, but I don't think they ever are prepared to deal with their parents' decision to separate. Hello, I wasn't ready for it either, but I'm an adult so should I have any excuses for tragedy? Although this guy had gotten a divorce rather quickly, like me, he seemed to get through it quite smoothly. He was dating again and really seemed happy. As for me, I really don't know if I will ever find that perfect relationship that will be good for me in my life. I'm still trying to figure out men in general, and why they act as they do. I'm sure they also wonder why we're from another planet too. Besides, I'm still trying to see if the two men that I have dated since my breakup will ever materialize into anything. I'm still not giving it much thought, especially now, since I'm exhausted all the time with my move. It's only 12 more days and a "wake up," as we used to say in the military. The clock is ticking, and my life is finally moving onward and upward towards what I want; at least I hope so.

So, now that it's almost been a year that's passed since my life changed forever, I now look back and realize people can be changed endlessly. Besides, who we've always been, can be converted from the inside out even though it's hard to convince ourselves of that fact sometimes. Being phony and/or fake may be easy for some because they don't live in the real world But, if one wants to share their experiences, church is a great place to share. For today, one of the pastors shared the fact why he was gone for a few weeks—his burn out, from working too hard, was affecting his relationship with his family. He took off for a few weeks too, I guess, to regroup and figure out his take on life. I know it helped him because today when I saw him in church, he looked so calm and collective.

I guess giving up the clutter in your life may make some feel like it's a loss in their relationship. So, what's worse, divorce or getting rid of that clutter? I guess emptying out your heart, as well as your mind, can be a good thing if it is done right. Getting rid of the bitterness, unforgiving ways, and bad friendships is another way to get right with yourself, your family, and with God. Moving onward towards what really counts is the key to success and emotional relief. I guess getting caught up in convictions and traditions can sometimes really get you going in a direction—be it bad or good is a question we must all figure out. For, it can hurt others, or it can hurt us—a lot.

Some may feel that asking for help is a sign of weakness, but can we always rely on ourselves for every chore, every complication in life, and every decision we make? Well, that would be a big fat, NO! Hello, I can't even rely on some of the day-to-day decisions on what to fix for dinner and even how to fix it. We get so caught up in our wants and needs that it's really a struggle sometimes; especially if a medical condition or other flurry of activity is thrown our way. Even if we think we know what to do and how to do it, the unforeseen is always there to interfere with our lives—just enough to irritate us. Right? Of course, it is. Now, think of life like this, looking back and dwelling on heartbreak may destroy you, but then you will be at a standstill. You will forever think what could of, should of, and would have been if you preoccupy those thoughts in your life. Remember; let go those horrid feelings by unhitching that trailer and parking it alongside the road. You don't need it anymore. Walk away!

I guess one of the challenges that I have come across since my divorce is how to persevere. Challenges come and go, whether you're single or newly divorced, but divorce seems to challenge us more than usual. The easy route is one that seems to be taken more often because people want to give up instead of pressing onward. Our feelings and emotions seem to rule our situation and those deep struggles we are confronted with tend to control our every thought. Do we have an answer to this dilemma? Well, I guess if we can get through it ourselves, we seem to have some control over our situation, and we can comfort others when our position is like theirs. Letting go and not trying to pull us out of this slump is the easy way out. By re-evaluating our past, we can move forward—really! New opportunities are always out there for us to grab onto, but we must be willing to jump into the pool without knowing how deep the water is at the bottom.

Ok, take my situation; in the last year my life has been in such turmoil that I'm surprised I'm still sane. My son got suspended from school, my ex and I fought with the school district, my ex had an affair then we filed for and then got a divorce, I wrote a book, I changed the looks of my current home with paint, bought furniture, my girlfriend and my mom thought they had breast cancer, my grandmother was in the hospital, I had a knee operation, the house I'm currently in is on the market, and I am buying a townhouse. Does this sound like enough grief? That would be resounding, YES! In addition, I am packing and cleaning out this current home to move next week—along with all the crap you must do to move. So, how am I keeping my sanity? I guess my short answer is that I'm looking towards the big picture. I can't look back or I would turn into a pillar of salt.

The future is what I seek and all it can offer me. I am going after all the things that were not available to me because I felt that "he" held me back when we were married. So, now a bright future can be mine. The wisdom that has held me together for this long will continue to be the glue that holds me together for years to come. My attitude is also one thing that has preserved me. I am a very positive person and look for the good in everything and everyone. It is a must! You cannot keep a bad attitude about anything in life or it will consume you, and it will be the harness that keeps you in one little spot and will not let you leave that comfort zone. Now remember that so you, too, can break free of your bonds.

My "new" life is just beginning. It may look like a marathon, but I must look at it as a sprinter would look at a race. I cannot look back or I will trip and fall. My eyes should always look forward to the finish line. For, if I look behind me, I will lose my momentum and my stride. I guess it's like being on a treadmill. If I look back, my face will be meeting the pavement quicker than I could imagine. My focus and my goals must be a priority for me now. Don't get me wrong, I still "trip up" and look back at the past, and sometimes it makes me mad; other times I feel like I have failed and failed terribly. I guess that's normal, but it happens; however, I only allow it to engulf my thoughts for just a few minutes. Then, I realize rather quickly that I was backsliding into a place that I didn't want to be—ever again. I can never let him have control of me, for if I do, I must realize where I could be headed. So, I should shake off these feelings and regain consciousness again. I don't want to go back there—not now, not ever!

I hate that feeling of helplessness and I can't let it control me. I've seen other women who have gotten divorced, and they just can't get out of that "funk" in their lives and continue to go back to that place—that horrible place, that is so familiar. I guess it's easy to fall backwards; it's just the focus of going forward that must have us in its grips. Just remember that the end of yourself is the beginning of your new life. We must replace fear with a vision. Living for something greater than what we now have can be our goal.

When we get to the point where we feel no one loves us, we need to remember that love doesn't keep a record of our wrongs. Well, think about it. Do we keep a record of all the things our children do that make us want to sell them to the cheapest bidder? Of course not! It happens, we address the issue, and then we move on. I mean, my son was 16 months old when he threw a toothbrush down the toilet, flushed it, and then screamed because he couldn't get it back. Think about that; if we always dwelled on what we could not prevent, where would we be now? That incident is something that I look back at and smile, but just shake my head. I don't dwell on that incident because there is no reason to do so. He also called 911 once when he was the same age, and I got a lecture from the local sheriff's department telling me that my son shouldn't have access to the telephone. So, what are you going to do? Did you ever hear, "Just deal with it!"

Sleeping and the morning chill never ceases to amaze me. With all that is going on in my life, I am getting very little sleep at night. All those restless nights mimicked last year when the divorce was nearing. I'm not sure if this "stress" is a good thing or not. I keep waking up in the middle of the night and cannot let my eyes fall back into that lullaby faze of the hour. Even this morning as I got ready for work, and then walked out the back door, I could see that rose bush I thought had died was now alive with fresh leaves of spring. I guess when you think something has died for good; there really is a little bit of life left. You must look a little closer than you did before. This rosebush is beautiful. It produces lavender roses with a sweet aroma. It is my favorite, and when I thought it was gone forever, I was a little sad. For, I had bought it, planted it, and then watered and fertilized it for the first summer after it was put into the soil. The results were remarkable! I had long stem roses perfect for my home.

I guess nurturing is an art form. When we care for our plants like we care for our relationships, they will thrive. On the opposite side when we stop caring, I think our hearts are hardened. Those feelings of remorse, happiness, and just "caring," are no longer alive within us and a part of our soul just dies. It's a sickening feeling that never seems to heal.

Today was another interesting day. I had my moving sale, and although it started slow, I did manage to sell enough items to buy myself a 50-inch flat screen TV. I just happened to get the last TV, which was last year's model and a display for less than $500. I was so proud of myself for accomplishing this feat. My ex would have never "let" me get something like this without his permission. Also, I went by my new place, and it looks like everything is nearing finality. The carpeting is in, and the hard wood floors are being sealed. The only other thing that needs to be done is the installation of the refrigerator. The frustration that I felt yesterday for everything that was falling apart seems like a bad memory from long ago. Is my life really getting back on track? Am I really getting on with my life to the point where I'm happy again? I thought I was happy last year when I was able to take a mini vacation by myself and really enjoy it, but now it's different. There is something new in my life where I feel so excited again and there's something I feel I really deserve. My ex was such an anchor in my life, and with every accomplishment I achieve, I have jumped another hurdle to get to the finish line. Each challenge I encounter, I try to face it without fear and without conviction of remorse. On that note, each decision I make and succeed at, I get a little closer to that satisfaction that I so desperately need.

I know that I have gotten further in the last year than I have in almost two decades, but do I really need another man in my life? As I drank a glass of wine this evening, I really felt a little lonely. I don't know if that relationship which started late last year is worth my effort, but when he's not around, I really do miss him. Is it the fact that he is the only one who has really paid attention to me that I truly need? Or is it that I really know, deep down, that he's really a compassionate person for which I never had in my life? Past relationships have touched me deeply, but none have affected me the way that he has in just a few months that I've known him. Now, that I've backed off from him, and informed him that I was still "friends" with the other guy I dated back in December, when he "dumped' me, he has opened just a little bit more. He has informed me about his past relationships more than before. This time he has volunteered information that I've always wondered about, but he has held deep inside. Is he now more trusting of me? Or is there something about him that says I will go away forever if I really go away for good this time? He's such a mystery to me. I want to know him from the inside out, but he has held back much about himself and will not share certain things.

I guess I always wondered about people who cannot share themselves with that special someone. Why hide the hurt you feel deep inside to others who want to be near you? Is there a steel door with an automatic gauge to close the entry of your heart when someone gets too close? Why does communication have to shut down when that special person in your life wants to know you further? The heart of a person has got to be a mystery. Blood pumps into and out of it to keep it strong, healthy, and to protect the other organs with life-nourishing ingredients, but when matters of the heart are concerned, it goes in the opposite direction. The rhythm changes; it now uses caution and protection with every question.

I think my stress level has started climbing down the mountain I have been on for the past year. Yesterday I had my walk-thru at my new town home. There were a few issues, but I was guaranteed that everything would be taken care of by my closing date in two days. As I laid in bed last night, I could feel some of the stress go away that has plagued me for what now seems forever. I can see the end of my journey, but also the beginning of my new life. By this weekend, I will be in my new home, and unpacking. I am so looking forward to a holiday weekend so that I can finish settling in—just imagine, last year at this time, I was miserable. Little did I know that my decision to confront my ex would lead me to a new chapter in my life? He really has given me freedom—I must look at those circumstances and try to understand why they happened. I have been given a second chance to move forward. I really can see myself in a different light now. A lot of people in my circumstances can't see life as I now do. I can only hope that they will be able to move forward like I am attempting to do.

9th Chapter

I have arrived, or have I?

As I look back today at the events of the past week, I have a smile on my face. Even though it seemed as if all my plans have blown up in some way, I have accomplished a lot. From the movers taking longer than anticipated, to the new appliances being scratched and dented, and then the phone, Internet, and cable couldn't be installed for one week; I have arrived at my new destination. I even found a new TV for less money than I anticipated. Even the newspaper wasn't delivered because they thought my new address didn't exist. I guess buying a place that is brand new can be a headache for all who think it doesn't exist, but today seems quite different.

I have a sense of accomplishment in my life now. With every glitch, I still made it to my destination with just a few bumps and bruises—literally. Just imagine that your life has been transformed forever in a way that has taken you to the ends of the earth. Along the way, you have encountered people, places, and events that have changed your thinking in some way. All the headaches, worry, and despair have taken hold of me in a way that I cannot dare describe to another. So why would this make you complete? Who knows? But will you make it further than you ever thought you would? Of course! When a game plan is put into action, it can have an amazing ending.

Take for instance today; my friend Jackie and her sons came over to my new digs, and I showed them around. She was quite taken back to where I now live as compared to the train wreck of a home I just left. She, too, is putting into motion a plan of her own to finally move out of her apartment and into a home of her own. She has a plan to pay off some bills and then look for a place she can call her own. She, like me, has pulled herself up with several bootstraps and has managed to preserve. Her ex is still a hot mess, but he is going back to school to make some use of his life, or so she hopes. His drinking became such a nightmare for a while, and while she struggled through his outrage, there will always be a part of her that will hurt forever.

But just think where would we both be if we refused to let go of our past? Not thinking a certain way anymore and allowing the past to be the past is a part of life that we must all go through, I guess. Some people may have it easier than others, but it seems like the victims have more to deal with than the victors. Besides, arguing with your ex about the past, or anyone for that matter, is something we all need to forget about. I know it's hard; I've been struggling with this myself for a long time; especially this past year. But I know from my attendance at church that God shall reveal to me what he wants me to do with my life.

When we fall, we think we've failed, but God wants us to progress and move forward towards him. We must stay with the pact and have the same mind set so we can succeed. Perhaps the best way to stay focused is to follow someone who has succeeded and set a pattern as they did. If we model our life after them, can we then be successful? Perhaps. I guess we just need to understand they too are human and can fail, but if we get up, dust off the debris, and then continue forward, we all have not failed, right? I guess it's the way you see a situation. Maybe we need to think of life as this—bad habits and bad morals will corrupt good people, but if we catch ourselves before we get there, we can change our situation.

Sometimes it can be easy to trust ourselves, but we may fall into a trap if we do this. We must trust a higher existence when we struggle—at least, I'm at that point. I had gotten away from religion when I was with my ex. I felt as if I had to hide the fact that I wanted to watch religious programs on Sunday. I remember changing the channel when he came into the room. Why did I do that? I now feel almost ashamed of myself for compromising my faith. I was not myself for the longest time. Looking back, I wonder why I did what I did when I was with him. I conformed to his ways of doing things and I didn't allow myself to be me anymore. What a waste of energy! His way was what I had morphed into over the years. The neglect I had allowed myself was not who I wanted to be. I was better than that! But now I am not looking back just to destroy my mind set, I am looking back to remember who I never want to be again! Changing my entire being didn't happen overnight; it took years of subtle changes to get me to the point of divorce. I think we both went through the same changes, but his changes were more distorted than mine. I still have my morals and values of what a "good" relationship should be between two people. He is now with a two-time cheater. Who knows when she will get tired of him and toss him to the side like she did her first husband or vice versa.

One thing we must remember about life is that others are always watching us. Our children, spouses, peers and friends see our actions and how we deal with life in general. So, being mindful of our dealings in life imprints a pattern. They see if we follow the majority, or if we plow our own path in life. Our successes and failures are a reminder to others that we can succeed in life, or it shows others that we are truly human. I guess presenting a life full of distorted values shows our children that they too can become like us, and it is ok for them to do so. Or it can also show them what not to do when they become adults. For example, my dad was an alcoholic. As for me, I am a social drinker, but my brother doesn't touch anything that contains alcohol. I guess we both saw what can happen to an individual who cannot control his actions—we both made our decisions as adults from his choices. As children, we both were traumatized by his illness that he never declared out loud. But as adults, we have learned from it and have moved on. We both have never blamed him for our trials and tribulations but have succeeded in what we want out of life.

Some children whose mom or dad are alcoholics are not so lucky. They can go one or two ways—down a good path, or down the path less chosen. I truly believe it is my strength and belief system, and my religion that has helped me. My ex was "force-fed" religion as a child, and to this day, he declares God as non-existent. It's a shame he can't deal with his past, as I have dealt with mine. I had a rough childhood too—never knowing if my dad would make it home from a drunken stupor was my main concern. But total relief would set in when I heard his truck come up the driveway. I hated him for what he put me through all those years ago. But since his passing nine years ago, I have felt relief that no one can again put me through this roller coaster. I feel sad that I had to go through those emotions, but it was events such as these that have made me a stronger adult.

I guess the best way to put it is who you worship is who you will become. For some people, worshiping earthly things is an important goal. Don't get me wrong; I like nice things too, but I don't put such a price on them as some might. I don't have to have my hair done by a certain hair salon, or a manicure by the prestigious business down the street. I just want a place I can call home that is safe from harm. I want a vehicle that is affordable and reliable so I can get to work. I have never wanted the "best" of anything, just good friends and family who are there for me in a crisis. Material things seem to be "worshiped" by some people I have known in my life, and it is a strange occurrence to me. I guess life is strange—following one's greed makes you comfortable. Just because it should be that way according to them, is something we should consider in our future actions.

With all the changes in my life, I still seem to have things that recur which still amaze me. Even the pastor at Sunday's service surprised me. He related to a house moving off its foundation to a rocky marriage that usually won't work. One in which the foundation is strong, and the house doesn't move is one that will survive. This was a dream I had late last year when I was going through my divorce. It really hit home and made me wonder why the connection was there. Also, I've had another dream lately that bothers me. It's about me and drugs. I can't remember exactly the sequence of events, but it has something to do with me being involved with drugs, but in the end, I make it out of a drug addition to survive.

I don't know why I now am having a dream like this. The only thing I can think of is that the marriage I was once in had its grips on me to the point I couldn't get out because I was hooked. I guess you could call me an "addict," or was I in such a familiar place that I would feel uncomfortable if I moved away from it? For me, divorce wasn't my ultimate choice, but I allowed it to happen. Now, I almost feel like I was forced into a different way of life, but as I look back, he really did me a favor. Even though it was tough, my foundation as a person has stood strong. By this, I mean that the strong storm that blew in against me has passed and I am now picking up the pieces and putting them where they should have been all along. My background was built on a rock—a firm foundation; it will stand solid. I may sway back and forth sometimes, but I will make it through this journey of mine.

I think the thing that has really helped me in my voyage this past year was my root system. By this, I mean a small tree is very vulnerable as a sapling, but by the time its roots have dug deep into the earth and grabbed hold of the rocks under the ground, it is now stable. It will survive the strong winds of a mighty storm. Just like us humans, if we look at our past experiences and how we have held firm with our convictions, we can make it through any journey.

We may forget that we cannot change past events. But holding onto it too firmly is another detriment to our being. We must accept it, let it go, and move on. It's only if we learn from it that we can grow. If we keep regurgitating it in our mind, we will never learn from our past; we will only be frustrated, with our feet firmly embedded in concrete. Maybe it's the fact that people forget they can't change the past. What's that old saying? "Build a bridge and get over it!" It's easier said than done, but it is so true. Another thing we should remember is that we can't change people, only ourselves. We must also self-examine ourselves before we dig deeper into a new life.

There was one thing that I noticed about my ex that made me worry about him. Yes, I said, "worry!" He held onto his problems so closely that he couldn't see anything else in his life. He believed that if he made lots of money, every problem in the world would melt away. His materialistic goals are going to be his ultimate demise. But I don't think he sees it that way—scary huh? Just as he looked at all the bad things that have happened to him in the past, he never had the time to look at all the blessings that were bestowed upon him in the present. There always seemed to be another problem in his life that frustrated him to the point of no return. Negativity was in the forefront of his every thought, and I believe this really affected him in several ways. He always wanted everything to be positive, and when it wasn't, he didn't know where to turn. Maybe that is why we used to have such one-sided conversations. There would be times when he just wanted to talk for an hour or two. This used to happen later in the evening when I was tired and didn't want to be bothered. I guess it worked both ways. I wanted to talk in the morning, and he didn't have time for me.

I guess growing apart is one way a relationship can end prematurely even with celebrities. I just read yesterday, June 1, 2010, that Al and Tipper Gore were separating after 40 years of marriage. Apparently, there was no infidelity; they had just grown apart. They were married in 1970; it is now 2010. It's almost like the oxen, and the mule yoked together—they both want to go in different directions, and neither will yield to one another. I guess it's like what the Pastor said at church on

Sunday. Allow your gentleness to come out in your life and be vulnerable by allowing it out to others around you. However, I truly believe that some people are so afraid of people seeing their flaws and imperfections that they can't go forward. They are so stuck in a rut that they can't show their vulnerability. They are too "comfortable" in their current situation that they are afraid of their future. They are only comfortable with their past because they are familiar.

Today I was up with my son. But, after taking him back to his dad's house later, I had a different feeling after driving away. Even though I am coming down from a high that I have been on for several months, I have a feeling of "completeness." The emotional stress I have been feeling for so long is now being put into a box and filed away in a closet. My emotional stress has calmed so much that I am now sick with a summer cold, but the accomplishments I have achieved are all around me. It's a feeling that I don't think I have ever had. I feel more confident with my situation and with myself. Even my ex and his mother haven't been in my place. It's as if I have gotten a power back into my life that was never there before. At my other house, it was as if they both would come into my home as if it were their own. Now, they are strangers to my environment; it's as if they are non-existent.

As I get settled into my new home, the calendar keeps turning. My son even asked me today if I was going to send his aunt, my ex-sister-in-law, a birthday card later this month. My first thought was why would I send a card to a person I never really clicked with and who now hates me? Her brother was the one who cheated on me, so why am I the "evil" one? She seems to be the one who went over to the other side when her brother changed his mind about his family. This is the woman who left me threatening messages on my voice mail, and who wanted me to do things for her after she totally ignored me for six months after he left. I don't understand why people can think this way and not care for others. Maybe that's why I need religion to keep me whole, and why they don't—for religion is not in their vocabulary.

I knew things were going too smoothly, because now my ex has done it again. He had the nerve to bring everything that was left in our old home together and bring it to my new townhouse and put it in front of my garage! I never thought he could go lower than he already had, but I was wrong. When I got home, there it all was, staring at me in the face. Even the Superintendent who is still working on the town homes beside me even made a comment. He couldn't figure out what was going on until I explained that my ex is not a nice person, and that is why he is my "ex." So, I did the only thing I could to irritate him back; I called the local police department on him. I asked the officer to call him and inform him that I will not put up with that action on his part. I don't know why he couldn't just put out everything for the trash this week! What part of him is so desperate to get back at me—I didn't have an affair, he did! Is he grabbing for straws and strength to put himself upon a pedestal? I don't understand why he is so out to get me. I've moved on. Does that bother him? I'm sure it does to the point that he hates me. I did it by myself. I went looking for a place of my own; I applied for the mortgage and put down my own money. I think my actions bother him; I really do. He is trying to make himself look like a big man, but all he is doing is making himself out to be the idiot he really is—deep inside.

I really wonder how his life is now. Is he truly happy with what he has created? He owns nothing but his truck and what can fit into it three times over. His truck is falling apart. His office is in "her" basement, and his paycheck is very little as compared to his big bucks he made just a few years ago. His ego has been bruised, and his wants are now many. So, how does a man go from having it all, to living with a "girlfriend" who provides almost everything? It must be a big blow for him to now find himself in such a precarious predicament. Is he afraid of me showing him that I can make it without his presence? I really believe this is part of his attitude. Because remember, he was the one who wanted me to stay in "that" house for at least another year. Hello! It was falling apart, and I had put some bucks into it already, but I wasn't about to continue that crap. Especially since it was in his name!

I've concluded that narcissistic people have no regard for anyone but themselves. Besides, I think my ex is their leader. Plus, it seems if they lose control of their emotions and their lives in general, they seem to lose all control. I've known people like this, and I've seen their tantrums. Their emotions run high whenever they are not in charge of their environment. They are like children who have been busted with their hand in the cookie jar. They scream, they yell, slam doors, and do everything to get their control back. They need that "in charge" feeling to make themselves feel better. However, all they do is look like idiots. Even though everyone around them can see how childish their emotions seem, the narcissistic person can't and won't let themselves see anything everyone else can see. It's as if everyone around them must tip toe around them to avoid their threatening ways.

As I look back, I am so glad to not be with him anymore. Even though I still have to "deal" with him because of our son, I hate having to do so. He will never change, and he will never grow up—in my eyes anyway. One day I really hope he finds himself. I hope he figures out what is important in life. Perhaps, an event will happen that will make him realize that money isn't everything and doing onto others as he would have done to himself is more important than material things he can acquire. Can he make it? I really hope so. He could be a great man, but with the path that he is currently on, I really doubt it.

The path of righteous is much better than the path of greed, but his darkened glasses cannot let him see the real world right now. I mean it's almost Father's Day. Remember that day last year when he moved out? This year my son will be in town, but I know he will remember rather clearly that this "holiday" was the turning point in his young life. In addition, it's almost the anniversary of the two of us filing for divorce. I can't believe it's been that long ago! This path has been long and hard, and it seems like the journey has just begun. I looked at the calendar and I just got sick. My stomach still churns from those emotions. I still remember how hurt and disgusted I felt when he admitted his actions. The loneliness is almost a distant vision, but truly it still walks beside me. Especially this week since my son is with his dad. I still wonder if my decisions have been correct. I still get scared of my life choices and where they will take me. Maybe if I knew, I could be calmer, but where would the fun be in that? I guess life needs to be an adventure, but sometimes I wish God wouldn't trust my instincts so much.

Life as it currently is still surprises me. My ex and I had a lengthy e-mail conversation yesterday on his actions and I ended up realizing why this man needed to be put on an island by himself with nothing to eat. His arrogance still seems to amaze me. I can't believe that he couldn't have just put everything from the last house out for the trash; I guess he wanted to make a point that "he" is still in charge. If he insists upon trying to make my life miserable, he's right on track, but I will not allow him to encompass my entire being.

Besides, he still—to this day, seems to think that his actions of adultery are justified. He even led to the fact that he has now found his soul mate and if she ever leaves, he'll go with her. Well, my comment is, "don't let the door hit you in the ass on the way out!" If he thinks that putting salt into an already open wound is commendable, he's confused.

Well, it's Thursday, four days after my ex decided to commit "stupid" again and leave all the crap from the last house in front of my garage door. Today is trash day, so I'm hoping the couch will disappear by this evening. I still can't believe he did that! I told my aunt about his actions, and she called him a juvenile. I think that word just about describes him. At least I had the dignity to just give him his things by either handing them to him or giving them to my son to deliver to him. He's still quite upset about my first book where I told the truth about our relationship. But, he doesn't care to remember the truth, so he's just a little troubled that his actions are spread around the world. Whaaah!

The weekend is drawing nearer to that one-year anniversary when everything started. Just think it's one year, 12 months, since all those around me noticed his cheating ways. How do I feel now? I think I'm angry, once again, at this point.

He has not learned his lesson. He still believes that he was justified in his actions and decisions. Personally, I think his life is in turmoil. No, I know it is. For yesterday, I found out that his sister has breast cancer. This has got to be eating away at him. She is only three years older than him, and I know he is now thinking about his own health. Don't get me wrong, he's had health issues a few months back, but now his sister is facing her own fears. At first, I felt sad for her, but after that initial thought, I didn't know what to think. Remember a few months ago, she was the one who wanted to institute a restraining order against me and sue me for my previous book that I wrote. Now her thoughts are with her own life.

So, how does one think of their existence? Do they look back at it with a smile and feel good about what they have accomplished? Do they look back at it and think that all the bad things they have put upon others was justified? Did they put themselves always first and others last—and truly believe this is what should have happened? I guess it's the way one thinks, is what should always be, or am I totally off?

Yesterday at church, "I am What I Think," was the topic of discussion. In that short period of time, the Pastor stressed that anxiety in our life creates depression. However, if we open our mind to a new way of thinking, anxiety can diminish. So, if divorce is always on your mind and the pressures of your children are the common thread between you, what can you do to alleviate your stress? I know that I sometimes sit and think about my situation and how I finally got to this point in my life. I don't beat myself up over every conversation and every fight with my ex. The contemplation is what keeps me seine, I guess. I try to constantly look at the good in my life—

not dwell on the bad even though I can't control what my son's father comes up with next.

It seems that my ex comes up with a new rule every week on what we need to do for our son, and then I should pay half of the expense. Spending time on that subject seems to deplete the air in my balloon! His thinking is so different than mine and we do not agree on the "ways of the world" according to Garth!

So, if you are what you think, do you then become that person? Proverbs 23:7 states that as a man thinkith in his heart, this is what they will become. This tells me that a person's thoughts can keep him or her captive. I guess it's like long-term memory; thinking about the same thing over and over allows your mind to easily retrieve that memory, but it will also make you miserable. The only answer is to think differently, and you can change your thoughts—right? Sounds simple, huh? Well, for some, thoughts never seem to change, they have only gone downhill towards more sin. This is my rendition of our marriage, and not his. He seems justified in cheating; I didn't get that memo—did you? If I were miserable with one man, why in the world would I go after another one who may do the same thing to me?

I guess at one time I really loved him—it felt like he was my soul mate, but as time wore on, I really started to see him differently. Even people around me couldn't understand what I saw in him because to them he was so chauvinist against women. I just ignored his attitude, but I should have run the other way a long time ago. I guess if we don't carefully look at ourselves and what we want out of life, our new way of thinking will never happen. I truly believe we should all be happy in a relationship. Respect between two people and others should be at the top of the priority list.

Next Course, Please?

Right when life has rounded that "one-year after the divorce" thing, my eyes have been opened once again. A conversation last night with a male friend of mine who has also went through divorce informed me of something that I had never thought of before. He said that when I was in my old home—that was originally with my ex—my son would always think it of "mom and dad's place." Now that I've gotten a new place, he will now think of it as "Mom's house" only. Whatever I do in this home will be because of Mom's decisions. Also, I guess, if I have someone over that I'm dating, and they spend the night, it's ok now because Dad doesn't have a say in that decision. I guess he had "ownership" in that old house in a way that I had never saw before. All the changes I made were without his dad, and were "against" his dad, so, he felt so much resentment that it hurt his heart. Now that I look back at his frustration and resentment against me, I truly understand where he was coming from in his actions. He wanted us to be a complete family unit, and when his control was melting away, he felt helpless and then tried anything he could to change it back to the way we once were even though his dad and I were miserable together.

I have to admit; I'm still new at this "divorce" thing. Each day there seems to be another incident that hits me in the face to make me wonder why existing can be so strange. Life goes a certain way for a long time, and then tragedy strikes. I recently talked to a friend about my current life, and his response was that karma was coming back to bite my ex. I'm not sure how I feel about that comment, but he may be right. It's almost like when you see a person getting away with "murder" for years, and then all those things they did are now being paid back full force. Everything bad that they did to others for a very long time is now coming back as revenge. Do they deserve this treatment? One can only wonder. Is there a higher plan to punish those who have always escaped by treating others poorly? Perhaps. As for me, I truly believe that we should treat others the way we want to be treated. For example, I was uncomfortable being around my ex-sister-in-law for years because I didn't feel like an equal to her. Also, she has no children of her own, so I guess she really doesn't understand how you must care for them on a 24/7 basis and how they are not perfect. I don't think she realized that she portrayed a certain image. The persona she exhumed about herself reflected a good image to lots of people. She didn't come from an "uppity" family with lots of money, but that seemed to be her goal—just like her brother—to have lots of money and to be able to do things that others couldn't. Don't get me wrong, they both are very driven to achieve that goal, but life has now gotten in the way of them achieving a perfect life. With her it's her illness; with her brother, it's cheating with another woman. So, are they both happy now? I really doubt it.

So, where do I fit in, in all this mess? Right now, I'm not sure. I just have to muddle through and try to understand them both in a way that is proper. I know I've said that I've forgiven him in my heart, but I guess I'm still awaiting that phrase from him, "I'm sorry." I know that I will never hear those words from his lips. Maybe that's why I lose it when he comes up with something else that sets me off. I've concluded that divorce does not stop when the ink is dry. It only continues until the tears come, again. Then, life persists onward.

Well, the construction continues on my townhome. The furnace wasn't properly hooked up, but it is now. My ceiling fans that I bought in May are now up and working. If I could only get my toilet to work properly, I'd be in a good position. Home ownership is quite interesting just like divorce. Last night my neighbor had his furnace cleaned out, and when mine was checked it needed the same thing. Between settling in, going to the dentist, and working on a disability claim, I'm tired. There are so many things that must happen, but it's a good stress—if you can call it that. I now have my own home, and I got it by myself. It's scary, but also an exciting time in my life.

As I look back on life, I have seen it go from a high to a low. My ex and his sister have also experienced the same. From making lots of money and taking vacations a few times a year, both are now dealing with medical issues, divorce, and a new life. I guess being on a "high" doesn't last forever.

My life has been very level recently, or maybe this is lack of a better word. As for me, I have gone on two nice vacations in Mexico in the past two decades, but I haven't really gone anywhere else. I guess my life has been simple, but I haven't dwelled on the fact that I've missed out. Sure, there are still things I want to do and go, but I don't feel that much resentment. I hope I never get to the point where I blame someone else for my failures. Maybe it's the occurrences in our life that make us think and love the way we do.

It's an interesting theory that our thoughts can control our decisions—many of which can be unstable. Our mind can take us to places where we never knew we could go before, and anxiety can follow us into every corner of our world. Just like reading a book—we can be transformed into a reality that we never thought could exist. Whatever we think can happen in our life; well, it really could happen if we allow it. It's garbage in garbage out, right? In my case, allowing the love in my life to think evil about me could have caused my ultimate demise, but I haven't let it. Just remember, our thoughts affect who we are, our children, and our friends and family. They can see us better than we can see ourselves, so maybe we should listen to them, huh?

Well, it's been three weeks and one day since I've moved into my new home. I am almost settled. The heavy boxes are almost empty, and I almost know where everything is located now. It's starting to feel like the home I should have been in a long time ago. My calm and peace of mind is returning even though my ex and I still disagree on many things.

It's been a year now since my ex left. Father's Day weekend is here once again, and the memories are still there. However, this year, I'm in "my" home versus "our" home. The same walls do not haunt me as before. The same experiences are not staring at me in my face as I go into each room. I think I've finally found some freedom in my life. As I look back upon this past year, I really wondered if my actions, words, and passion really was valid. It only hit me today when I talked to a neighbor who also has an ex-husband. She even validated my thoughts on the furniture that my ex and I had bought together. Memories are attached to furniture like stains are embedded in clothes—they never seem to go away. You could even give them away or throw them out. It may help your psyche but not your pocketbook. Sell that crap! I thought I was the only one who felt that way, but I guess not.

All the passion and effort that I put into that old house to wipe away the bad thoughts of my life were never meant to go away unless I moved or sold them at a yard sale. That old furniture has changed my mind about a lot of things. I really have felt a release of emotions that have needed to go away for a long time. In my experience, it seems women think a lot differently than men when it comes to this subject. Men tend to think with their pocketbooks and women with their heart. Men think that it's just "furniture." You know, something to sit on, put your feet on, or sleep on. It seems that they think no emotional value has been placed upon it, and it never will have any value in that respect. My thoughts were if I at least sell it and get some monetary value, I have succeeded in my quest. My goal was to delete those bad memories from my past. Men think we're wasting our money and our time. Getting rid of my wedding rings was one of the first things I did last year. Even though I got very little from their value, I released my confused emotions to the point that I was in charge again. I needed to manage just a miniscule portion of my life—a point where I could feel good about "me" again. I'm sure my ex still has his wedding ring; something just tells me that he won't get rid of it, because he's either waiting for the price of gold to go up, or it's not a priority in his life right now.

It seems my ex took so much confidence with him when he left. It's taken me almost a year to get just a portion of my confidence again, but it's working. I've gained so much of my life back, but I still feel I need to keep on that path to heal my emotions. Will I ever get back to my life that I once knew? God, I hope not! I just need a life that can make me feel important and fulfilled once again. I want to feel complete, and not estranged in my thoughts and actions. I need to complete myself fully, and then I can add someone new to my life. This person must also feel the same way, and we must be on the same path of life, or it will end as before.

Well, today is Father's Day—exactly one year ago, my eyes were puffy and red with sorrow. I was sleep deprived and emotionless when my former husband came over to move his stuff out of our home. Today, on the other hand, I went to church with my son and listened to a sermon about being content with your life. Being pleased with yourself is being satisfied, right? I guess it's a big difference from one year to the next—with my life anyway. I guess if you look at life from the time I was born, I must look at my "learned" behaviors. The last two decades I've noticed that our learned behaviors lean us towards being creatures of habit. Society has pushed us towards catering to a lack of commitment to everything, and if we don't like something, we can take it back and return it for something new. Even marriages seem to be heading down that path—our pets are more loving and dedicated to us than our significant other. Scary, huh?

By not being happy and working on our relationships, we are showing our children how to dispose of it and get a new one—sometimes rather quickly. Is this our new norm? Besides, how do we control our needs and wants in a way that teaches the next generation to respect life and relationships? Do we look to God for guidance? I know I must go in that direction to be content in my life. It's a fulfillment that takes me to a level of not wanting to be greedy. I guess you could think of it this way, the more money we make, the higher the lifestyle we choose to have. Personally, I have gotten to the point of wanting to just pay my bills and be able to put some money in the bank for retirement. My ex had always wanted to travel and did not want material things. The more he traveled, the more he desired to go to more places. Sure, I'd like to travel more too, and it's a goal—eventually. However, I am not dwelling on it right now, and it doesn't make me sad that I can't go to those desired places. I don't feel that I must travel to make myself feel "whole." Friends and family are my most important assets right now. I want to be with them as much as possible—they make me feel content.

I am one year and a day away from remembering my trip to the courthouse with my ex to file for our divorce. What a difference one year makes! I'm not sure how I'm feeling right now. It still seems so new—364 days have flown by and I'm not sure where they went. My routine has drastically changed, and now I'm responsible for my own bills. I think it hit me the other day when I got my first bill for my mortgage, which is due in less than two weeks. I'm excited yet scared; I'm ecstatic but cautious.

Where do I go from here? What part of life trained me to become my own person and be at this point in my life? If I knew, I'd probably smack that person! For, this life is still unfamiliar even though one year has come and gone. Are the songs on the radio still there, you know, the ones I heard when it first happened? They now have a special meaning. However, the stigma of divorce isn't so prevalent now. However, that word still haunts me—you know, "Divorce," and my learning process continues to change.

As I sit here in my kitchen pouring my thoughts into this book, I look out my window and watch the construction workers in the next building complete the last structure in this area. It's a building consisting of five townhouse units and in just a few months, they'll be completed. I guess divorce isn't like construction; it's a continuing process that never seems to end. In construction, there is a beginning, middle and an end. Soon, all the workers will have gone to the next site, and this site will be a distant memory. They will look back as they drive by and say to themselves that they were a part of that project. I guess marriage and divorce can be considered a "project" too. It must be carefully planned, and the ultimate destination is a happy life, but not always. What you put into your "project" is what you will get out of it. If it is something near and dear to your heart, you will be carefully neutering it. But, if you care less about your outcome, it will only leave bad memories—perhaps forever. It's like being in a relationship just for the ride and to profit from it somehow. It won't last and it will go down in a blaze of glory in the end. I guess a construction project and a marriage are more similar than we want to admit.

Well, today I have reached one more milestone in my life. Today, one year ago at 4:30 p.m., I met my ex at the courthouse, and we filed our paperwork, together, to end our marriage. I'm not sure what I'm feeling today, but part of me is numb. That part of my life with "him" is gone. The house has been sold, but we're still fighting. Why does divorce have to be so devastating? Plus, why do we still look back at our past lives and feel regret or remorse for the things that are out of our control? What we could control, did we really control? Or was that other person hindering our movements so much that we didn't want to progress at all, so we wouldn't hurt their feelings? Life gets so complicated sometimes that I just want to throw up my hands and scream! How about you? I guess the thing that makes us keep going is that there is something better out there for all of us, we just need find it, right?

Nap Time

I've now been in my new home for almost four weeks. Somehow, I've realized that I must have been wound up for so long because now I can't get enough sleep, nor can I get enough rest. I go to bed totally exhausted and wake up the same way. I am sleeping through the night for the most part, but my body has given out on me and now I'm in unfamiliar territory. I've been tired like this before, especially, when I went to night school for two years straight. However, I cannot compare both instances, but I guess there was a goal in mind with both situations. I wanted to better myself and nothing would get in the way of my goal. Comparing both times of my life makes me look back in awe. How did I do it without losing my mind? How did I keep going? Somehow, I want to answer those questions, but part of me doesn't want the conclusion. Both times caused me to re-evaluate my life and my goals. My drive was intense, and my body just went along for the ride.

Today, June 25, 2010, marks another anniversary. Today, one year ago, Farrah Fawcett and Michael Jackson both died. It was an eventful day—and an eventful week. Also, my co-worker Mary found out about her ex-husband's extracurricular activities one year ago, when he was cheating on her. It seemed that the world was falling apart last year at this time. Even Ed McMann died this same week. I don't even know how we all made it through this series of tragedies. I think I was frozen in time, and everyone followed me down that path. It was as if my life was falling apart and I had nowhere to turn, and the rest of that week was near my skirt tails, following my every move.

I think my subconscious led me for the rest of that year and up until this point. Plus, my thoughts and ideas that I learned from childhood have served me well and I think that is how I survived. Oh, believe me, I've had my moments of complete sorrow, but I've also had my times of total and complete happiness. But isn't that what life is about? We're really not prepared for the sorrow in our lives, but happiness comes a lot easier, right? Our troubled times have opened our lives to realize how things should be because when we are content, that little "happiness" cloud follows us everywhere. On the other hand, that little black cloud just over our shoulder makes us miserable, or does it? I guess it's the way we look at life, for if we think we will be miserable forever, it will happen. If we look at what a "good" life brings, we can make it through our moments of sorrow, or can we?

Well, I made it through this first week after Father's Day, and I have survived. I still don't know where I will end up in life because many things are still uncertain. I have returned to the one guy I met last September, but was it a mistake? Because, yesterday he asked me why I didn't see the other guy that I dated for about a month back in December of last year. Does he want reassurance that he is the one I want to be with? Or does he still need me in some way, and he has to have that much-needed pat on his back to reassure him of my intentions? However, he seems to want to be with me only when he fits me into his schedule. The other guy did that too; not again! However, both are similar in one way, they want to help others, and they don't allow themselves a relationship to encompass their world. Everyone else around them is more important, and I am there to fill the gaps when they are lonely. Or is it the fact they are bored, and a female fits the bill? I guess I don't really understand either one of them.

Why do men get to the point where they need to fill themselves up with everything but a relationship? What has brought them to this point? Maybe it's the fact that men handle divorce differently with woman. All women want to do is scream and bad mouth our ex's; right? From what I've seen, men repress their anger and their emotional crisis, to only throw themselves into activities that take them away from their pain. Will they ever get to the point where they don't want to grow old alone? Besides, will I ever be available when they are? I guess timing is everything?

So, while my life goes on each day, am I doing what I am called to do? Am I putting myself into a position that is new and tailored to my new goals in life? Do I have a vision where I must go, or will I perish before I get there? Not knowing where you are going can make one let go of those goals and give up. I do know one thing about life; God must be in my decision process and in my growth so I can carry onward. My sanity and destiny depend upon it.

Life has dealt me many cards this year and my move brings so many changes. Finally, I have something that is totally mine—mortgage and all. All I want to do now is just throw up. Why, you ask? Well, think about my last year. I've had so much pandemonium in my life for 365 days, however, now it's finally settling down. Maybe I was so used to things going wrong that when things are finally going my way, I'm not sure how to handle it. I have my own home! Wow! The mortgage is more than what I was paying on the old place—but I can afford it. Things are now different. It may not be the Ritz Carlton, but it's not the Projects either. It's a quaint little place that has my name on it—literally. I'm still scared about the payment, but God is on my side, and I've noticed a big difference in my life since I went back to church. I am now really enjoying my life more, and with his help, I am managing my bills, and my sanity. Sounds a little strange, huh? I don't know what it is, but a co-worker said something to me the other day that made sense. She said that when you contribute financially to the church, you seem to be able to make it financially in your life. Guess what? She's right. Even though I can't contribute every week to the church, I've seen a big difference in my life in just the past couple of months. I want to give more, but I also need to make sure I can pay my bills. I give what I can and that is all my church asks. I'm glad I attend a service that doesn't guilt me into taking more of my money than I can afford. But shouldn't it be that way? Of course!

Well, here again, when you think life is going your way, life throws you another curve ball. My friend Jackie's ex is at it again. Now he's trying to attack my character. He thinks I am making his life difficult now. It's complicated, so I won't go into the details. I don't think I have been so upset—ever! I was so upset that I drank too much wine that night, and I felt really bad the next day—I even got physically ill. I'm glad I had the day off. My neighbor sat with me at the kitchen table that night to hear my story—we both needed to vent, I guess. With my bad day and then another argument with a family member, I was ready to lose it. I think she was too. Her son is with her ex on the east coast for the summer, and with all the crap he's pouring into their son's ears, she's ready to scream. They've been divorced for three years now, and she thinks her ex is acting like the hero to her son. Or is her ex trying to be the complete connection that her son doesn't currently have?

So, why do I think men can't handle being alone? In all of my years of seeing divorces and men losing their wives due to their death, I've noticed that men can't be unaccompanied. They seem to be yearning for another relationship, but sometimes they just don't jump on board with that idea. The only exception to that statement is the two men I've dated since my ex left. Both have engrossed themselves into projects, volunteering, and into their families. They even travel for work so much; they don't even have time for a relationship. Has this "illness" made us all into a group of people who can't make decisions and also scares us into staying single for the rest of our lives? I think not. I have two relatives who have been married four times each! Really! Even one of them, a cousin, is the same age as me. How did that happen? I'm not sure if I'm up for that much baggage! I mean, doesn't everyone deserve to be happy? That even includes my ex, I guess. But I guess the happiness gene needs to be real and the relationship has to start out with the truth. That's what I want, but will I ever get it? Take for example the guy I've seen on and off for eight months. I've never met any of his friends nor his family. He says that the men would flirt with me and the women would be jealous. What the hell does that mean? He's Latino and I'm white—big fat deal! He needs to get off that jackass mentality because it is going nowhere fast!

People have so many ideas about other people and their lives. For instance, my dad was extremely judgmental when I was growing up, and I hated the way he thought. But, as for me, I see everyone as equal. If you're a jerk, you're a jerk, I don't care about your skin color or that you think differently. My ex is white; the guys I have dated are Latino, and what I like to call a "Heinz 57" mix since he's Black, White, Asian, and Native American. Maybe I wanted to meet someone who was totally opposite of my ex. Was I totally against White men—no, not really? But I'm totally not ruling out men of other ethnic races. I want to get into the depths of their soul. I want to know that they are good people who would go out of their way for someone—and not do for just themselves. I've already been through that crap! They also should want to be with me and make time for "us."

As for my ex, he seems to think his current relationship is perfect now—for his sake, I hope so. He never made the same time for us like he does for her. Somewhere along the way, we went down different paths and that became our demise. I want to be at that point of my life one day where I'm bored—well, just a little. Sounds crazy, but something needs to settle down and soon.

Today I feel a little better. My energy is still lacking, but I know I will get better. It seems like I've had so many incidents this past year that have taken away from my sanity. I've had to fend for myself a lot more than I signed up for in this lifetime. I really could have used more than one hug lately. I've had many times recently where I just wanted to crawl in a hole and cry so hard that my soul could be cleansed. Maybe it's the fact that everyone needs a soul mate to inform you that the bad times will eventually go away. Even my doctor is dating. I saw him yesterday and I was amazed how calm and collected he has become. I even commented that he looks happy now. Don't get me wrong; he's still dealing with his ex and all her grief, but now he has another person in his life to help him through the rough times. I want to feel that way again. I want to have someone with me, and really with me, to have productive discussions, and someone to hold me when I am at my weakest.

I don't think anyone can be strong all the time; there will be times when soft words and being in someone's arms are what we need to make it through each day. I miss that feeling. Even lying on the couch next to the one who means the world to you while watching a movie is well worth the wait. It's something that sounds good to me right now. The pit of my stomach is so empty, and extreme loneliness has come back to haunt me yet again. It's as if that feeling never really left, it was in the back of my mind waiting to attack me again when I was helpless.

Lately, vulnerability is my middle name. I hate feeling this way. I even feel lonely when my son is with me, not to mention being in a crowd. I had this feeling last year when my son and I went to the Renaissance Festival. We were watching the jousting match, and as I looked around, all I could see were families and couples enjoying themselves. There I was, in a crowd of people, but I was all alone, at least that's the way I felt. Will I ever get that "complete" feeling back again? Will I ever have calm in my life again? God, I hope so. I hate feeling this way. I'm not the kind of person who wants to be alone forever, and right now it doesn't feel good. My heart feels like it has been ripped out of my chest once again, and it hurts—a lot.

Another holiday is now upon me, another time for reflection. The 4th of July should be a happy time, right? Well, it out started that way—well, not really. The pit of my stomach still aches. My loneliness gene is still here to haunt me. Now, I feel as confused as when my ex left last year. The chaos in my life has come back full force and I feel so distraught—I am strong for the most part, but once again I have been broken.

I need to grasp hold of something that can make me tough again. My prayers to God are being heard; I just know it. So, I now await an answer, a direction to keep me going down the path to happiness. Aren't all things held together with God's help? Isn't he ultimately in charge of your life? Do we need to be going through what we are going through at this moment in time, to get to the other side—the other side with the bright light? I don't think I will ever know the true answers to these questions, but I know I have gotten the strength I need just by asking for it. The higher power surrounds us all; we just must reach out for it and trust that it will surround us like a blanket to keep us warm.

So, what now? Do we ever get to the point that we will ever trust again or even love again? I think I've asked that question once too often in the past year. Why won't this emptiness ever go away? Or does it ever go away? The closeness of another person is something that can be missed more in one's life than you can realize. Being alone is something that can make or break you. I thought I could be stronger than I am, but I have my boughs of grief. It's not just sorrow; it's deep down hurt that goes to the bottom of my spirit. It can't be tossed aside so easily this time. Will it ever be? When will I regain my strength again? Besides, my grandmother is not doing too well, one more thing to consume me. When will it all stop, and my life can resume to normal? I guess I don't have a grip on reality, nor do I have a grip on life. My faith is the only thing that keeps me sane. I want to be happy in my life again, but when will it ever return? When is it my turn to be normal again? When can I empower myself so I can feel that sense of calm I once had? I am awaiting the answers so I can live again with peace in my heart.

I even try to keep it together when my son is with me. But, as soon as he goes to his dad's, I find myself reaching for a tissue to wipe away the tears. My strength is the only thing that I allow my son to see. I must be strong for him, so he can see a parent in control. I know he hates being with his dad, for he has told me that his dad's girlfriend is a person he does not respect. I know he still blames her for what has happened. The trust he once had for his father has been shaken. Will he ever get it back? Will he ever trust in his own relationships? I hope one day he will realize what is important in life and follow that vision.

Tomorrow, I will go back to work; now I can concentrate and keep my mind off the hurt and pain which still exists. How can I escape this emotional roller coaster? I wasn't truly content because all around me are disturbing consequences. I can't run and I can't escape. Am I at the point where I can't get away? I thought I was heading towards success, but right now I don't know. I'm not normally this distraught, but all around me are people pounding me into the ground and I have no say in what they're doing. I don't think I've been this sad for a long time. I have tears in my eyes that won't fall down my cheeks. But tomorrow is another day.

The sun has risen once again this morning, and I'm sure it will fall this evening. Birds will soar in the air, and cars will drive on the highway. My feelings of despair will need to heal before I can go on with my life. I'm not at the point where I don't want to live anymore, so don't get me wrong. I am just at a very sad, lonely point of my life that only time will heal. I guess it's like that old saying, "God only gives you what you can handle, but I wish he didn't trust me so much!" It's very true today.

I've seen people at their lowest point, and after a while it's like PTSD. You become numb to hurt and pain. You don't have any emotions anymore towards anyone, and basically you don't care about people and their issues. I don't want to be like that. At one time, I wanted to be a counselor because I really care about people and want to help. But, right now, people and their issues are something I don't care to deal with at all. I have my own issues to deal with; and I'm not at the point today to help anyone else. I guess I must believe that God has a plan for my life, and that I can handle all that is thrown at me. But no, I'm so tired—both emotionally and physically. All the alcohol in the world can't fix me, so I won't go there. I just must trust that my faith will get me to Round 2. Hopefully, this round will be better than the first one.

I've reflected on the past four days and have concluded that life is changing all around me. Even being at today at work was tense. I want my life to take another turn, but to where? Life seems to be evolving around me, but am I ready for it to take me to the next level? There is still, to this day, so many questions and very few answers to my needs and wants. Where do I go from here? I feel like a toddler taking my first steps in the world. Each time I move, will I fall? Or will I get closer to my goal? Besides, what is my goal now? Will someone tell me, or do I have to guess this time? Was life so simple back then as compared to now? There I go again—asking too many questions, which yield very few answers. Sure, I could ask for help, but will I get it this time, and from whom? That bottomless pit in my stomach seems to be my guide these days. I thought it was gone for good, but it's like a bad penny—it keeps coming back. I don't even know if a significant other could get me through this one. The weight of divorce is still taking its toll on me, and I don't know if I will ever get through it. Wasn't it supposed to be done by this time? I mean, it's been over a year since he left, but the emotional toll has hit me so hard, and it won't go away. Maybe it's restlessness. Maybe it's the fact that I miss being a part of someone else's life—no matter how bad it was? Sounds crazy, I know, but I guess sometimes we put up with crap that we really shouldn't have to just for the convenience of being with someone. I look back at that now and think how I must have been crazy to want to be with a man who bad-mouthed me behind my back, and never wanted me around. Well, he finally got his wish to be shed of me, because he has moved on without me into another cheater's arms. Will he really get his hope for that new life that he wanted all along? I guess only time will tell. I really do hope he gets what he wants and needs—he's been searching for a long time. I'm not sure why he did what he did to me, but life for both of us will never be the same. I think we really hate each other for what we think the other did; however, we must be cordial to each other, or we will drive each other crazy. I know that I want a life full of love and kindness—don't we all deserve that?

My heart seems heavy these days and my emotions seem to be overloaded. Every minute I want a hug. I need someone to hold me tighter than I've ever before held. I want intimacy more than one could ask for—why? I don't know. Is it because that one-year mark is almost upon me? I've got more than two months until that eventful day last year that ended my marriage in divorce court.

How am I going to make it by myself until that eventful day? Do I now try to prove that someone will still want me? Do I attach myself to every man I can find because of my ex's indiscretions? Do I engross myself into a project that makes me forget my troubles like I did last year with the painting project in my last house? Do I focus all my energy in my job? I'm not sure in which direction I should go. I am lost, all alone and unsure of my future—STILL! How do I proceed? I so desperately want to tell someone who can comfort me, but no one exists who can accomplish that task right now.

So many thoughts race through my mind all day long. Have I made the right decisions lately? How have my decisions and those of his dad's affected my son? I wish there was a handbook, filled with all kinds of answers, that comes along with your baby when you leave the hospital, but it doesn't work that way. I also need a handbook for the newly divorced! The guess the other thing that still bothers me is what do I do about a love life? On the other hand, should I even worry about one? Since I just ended a "part-time" relationship, AGAIN, of which I never really felt a part of, do I now go out looking for a relationship with a guy who really loves and needs me? Or do I go back to a relationship that only existed one-month, late last year? At this point, I don't know where to turn. Confusion is a total part of my concentration, and it is making my life miserable. There were issues in that relationship too, so I'm not sure if that one would work either.

Men are starting to drive me crazy once again, and as I said before, the trip is very short! I hate feeling out of control. I just don't know if I was ever in control now that I think about it. Events were happening all around me, and I have been pulled in so many directions that it's a blur. One year has passed since he left, and I'm still struggling to keep afloat because I feel that sometimes I am drowning in my own thought process. Men seem to oversee their life but don't include me in it for some reason. I've just been through a relationship where I wasn't included even though I thought I was a part of someone's life that meant something to both of us. I don't want to make that mistake again, you know, the promise of a relationship, but not really. My goal must be to find someone who really knows where they're going, have the "stuff" they need—both physical and emotional—but they need a partner to go with them. Let's hope that man exists!

Well, it's another day closer to the weekend, and I don't have my son this week, so I have freedom. I want to go out, but with whom? If I don't keep myself busy, I feel like I'm missing out on something. Is this the fallout of divorce? Is keeping busy a must because if you don't, you'll go crazy? It seems like I have kept busy for a long time now, but has it helped? Still, there are so many questions in my mind. As a friend once said to me, "The first year of a divorce is a trip!" I wonder why he said that. Perhaps it was the fact that he's been through it too, but a very long time ago. Mine is still very fresh in my thoughts. I sometimes even wonder what my ex thinks about this whole situation and what he put me through. This thought only comes to my mind for about five seconds, and then I come back to reality and realize that he doesn't care what he put me through. It seemed it was all about him, and what he wanted. But that's my take on the situation. I guess we both did things wrong, but who was more "wrong" than the other? In my mind, his adultery was the last straw, and

I couldn't continue from that point onward. I just wonder whether he will ever see that his actions were against the vows of God. Gee, there I go thinking about him having core values! What was I thinking? I guess values are something that you either conform to or not. Whether or not if it is important to you, is something that you are born with—I must believe that thought or else I think I will go crazy.

It's the weekend again, and many thoughts are going through my head. Will I be alone like this for the rest of my life after my son leaves the nest? I have my neighbors and friends who surround me, but will it be enough? There's a hole somewhere in my heart and I'm not sure how to deal with it. The impact that this divorce has had upon me seems to always be in the back of my mind and it won't go away. There's a part of me that feels insignificant, and another part that sees this freedom as an expression that I've needed for a long time. My newly found independence has brought forth many questions, but no one seems to have the answers for me. So, I guess when my son really does leave home for good, where will I be? Is there really someone out there for everyone like the old saying goes? Time will only tell me these things but not until I'm ready, I guess. I have seen people get divorced and they can move on quite easily, but others have more difficulties. I guess we all have one thing in common—we all survive somehow, and loneliness and grief is just a part of our daily lives. So, are we at the point of being abandoned? It has crossed my mind once or twice. I guess keeping busy is one thing we all think will "fix" the issue. The same problems and successes that were meant to happen do happen. It's the way we go about dealing with them that counts in the end.

As I think about this past year, I am still at the point where I don't want to deal with this mess, and yes; it's still a mess. Sometimes I just want to run away and put my head in the sand. Other times I feel so empowered that I could conquer the tallest mountain. It seems like the down times are the ones that are so critical to our psyche, though. We must think rationally, or we will break apart into the ocean like the Titanic and never survive the cold ocean water. Only those who refuse to let their heart die will make it to the next point in their lives.

Many things remind me of where I am in my life right now. Such as, I am here now at my kitchen table looking out the window at the new townhouses still being built. The windows are in as well as the garage doors, but inside the "guts" of each unit is still empty. There's no drywall, no flooring, and the list goes on. I guess it's like my life—the physical structure is there, but there's something missing inside of me and in my life, but I'm not sure what it is. In each unit, the windows are installed, but you can look through them and see the other side. Is that the way I am being viewed by others? Can everyone but me see where I am at this point of my life? I look sturdy enough, but inside there's no building blocks and no solid walls to firm up my foundation. Everyone can see my demise, or can they see that one day I will be sturdy inside too? So, I have to get through this first year. Then, and only then, can I have what I need to go forward because I have been made whole? I have periods of doubt, believe me, and it's not a pretty site. I need to believe that I can make it on my own again—without a soulmate, this has to happen!

Reflections

Having a soul mate is something that would be nice to have, but not something I have to have. I could be on my own, but deep down, I don't want that for myself. I guess I long for that special person in my life to share memories and special times. For example, I was reminded this morning at church that there doesn't have to be a perfect soul mate to make a perfect life happen. A guest speaker who was in a wheelchair began by explaining why he was in that chair. He was diagnosed at seven years of age with a rare muscle disorder that makes him very weak. Plus, he must hold up his head with the support of his arm. I was amazed by how composed he was, and his story was even more fascinating. He was now an adult, married with a good job and with two little girls not quite in elementary school.

I know with his disability he's had to overcome obstacles that I could never even imagine. However, he has not let it hinder his ambition to prosper and to move forth with his life. With every word from his lips, I got the impression that his joy for life and for God has prepared him for whatever may come his way. He has gotten busy doing the work he was meant to do. I have learned that the power of pursuit and determination can change your life whether you're dealing with a disability or going through a divorce. What an inspiration!

There was also another thing he mentioned that really hit home. Due to his disability, he can't pick up his children. However, when they were little, he compromised and got down on the floor and played with them by rolling across the floor. He was bonding with them in a way that they understood. I guess that's what I need to do with my son more than I ever have before. He's 14 years old now, and the time will pass so quickly from now until he's out of high school. Even though I need my space too, I never felt like I got it since he's been born, because I had to be there for him in every way. His teenage years are preparing him to become an adult. His dad and I are the ones who must set examples for him to grow into adulthood. Although I feel his dad has shown a side of himself that I never want my son to repeat, it is a good lesson for his growth.

Everything we touch and feel, along with the people we meet will influence our thoughts and goals. We must filter out what is good and what is bad so we can grow towards a life of good. God has taught us how we should act, but do we always do it? Of course, not—that's why we are human, right? Must we always have that stamina in our soul to succeed? I know I need it, but some days, it's not there. I mean, how do we want to be remembered in our old age? Shall we let our children see us as weak or should they watch us struggle? I guess a little bit of both are good for their growth as well as our own. I guess life presents us with so much grief sometimes that happiness is overrun with self-doubt. Don't we all want to be happy all the time? Well, if we were, we would never realize all those bad moments in our life can go away—even if for only a few minutes, hours, or even days.

I guess our legacy is what we will present to our children, and how they deal with it will either make or break them. How we prepare them for life and what we hand down to them becomes our job as parents. As adults with divorce in our past, we must also prepare ourselves to live to the fullest. The message we send to ourselves must also be given to our children. Going forward and prospering is how we must think. We must grow our prior events into something positive, for if we don't, we will fail and fail badly. We must pursue and love people genuinely—for our endurance demands it. We should surrender ourselves to that next opportunity that will present us with greatness. We must leave nothing undone to fix ourselves for we have to get to Phase 2 of our lives. No one gave me a manual for this part of my life, so I must figure this one out for myself.

It's Monday again. It's another day to excel, right? Well, I can only excel if I wake up. It was a short weekend, and I didn't seem to get much sleep. I guess the world keeps revolving around me even though I'm not ready for it to do so. I even went to see a former neighbor yesterday, and the lady behind her whose husband died from a brain aneurysm last year seems to be moving onward. She sold their truck and camper, and then painted, and re-caulked the house. She's also doing some concrete work on their front driveway too. Is she like me trying to "change" things in her life to regroup? It seems like that's what I did to forget, but it didn't work. The memories were still there, and they haunt me every day. I can't escape them because they were embedded into the walls, and they would stare at me when I turned my head. There was one difference though, she completely lost her husband, I still have my jerk to deal with about everything regarding our son. Did she luck out by her husband leaving her life via death? Sometimes I wonder what would have happened if her life was my own.

I could relive my life through others and wonder about all the "what if's," but what would it accomplish? Would I feel any better if he were six feet under or as he is now? Things would be different. He would leave me with all the parenting responsibilities and expenses. Plus, I would be making every decision without his approval. He would miss all the opportunities to see our son grow up and mature. Every major event would be missed, and I would be the only one attending each one. But I know one thing—my son would be cheated by this scenario as well. Even though his father is an adulterer, it wouldn't matter to our son. He would miss his father in a way that I do mine. My dad had his faults, but I do in some ways miss not being able to talk to him. It's weird now, because I don't even remember what his voice sounded like, for he's been gone for almost a decade. I, with all the others, have survived but have our lives been fulfilled or have they been lacking something? Or will we ever know what the outcome would have been with the people we have lost?

Life gets interesting some days. The weather can fluctuate, your children can drive you crazy, but one thing that will never change is your attitude about living. When horrible things are presented to you, there are two decisions you can make. Either you can pull yourself up and go on with something you've lost, or you can lie down and die. Is this a tough decision? Probably. But what other choice do you have? I mean, Mary is still struggling from her split last year. She's letting her kids tell her where they want to live, and she's letting her ex still influence her emotions. I guess I'm just as guilty even though I haven't talked to my ex in about three weeks. In reality, I'm glad not to speak with him; because his emotional control is still there—if even just a little. He can still push my buttons, but now I keep a little magic bullet in my back pocket. I have made the decision not to let him tell me what I should do—because now I am not his puppet! Really? Does he still think I will do what he says, just because he says to do it? Do I lie down, roll over, and die just because he says so? Well, duh! I don't think so! I guess many people; when divorce enters their lives, just fall apart. I was there for just a short while, but now my strength has returned. This reminds me years ago of a friend whose husband went to Iraq. He ended up cheating on her with a co-worker, and then e-mailed her that he had met someone and wanted a divorce. She told me that she cried for three days, but then she pulled herself up, dusted off the remains of her marriage and then made some decisions about her future. He ended up coming back with the new chick, and she gave up custody of her two boys for just long enough to go back to school and make something of herself. Was it hard for her? Of course, but the choices that we must make because of others' decisions are ones that are not easy, but very necessary. There is something better out there for us, but we must want to pursue it for ourselves. Maybe if we put our children in front of our decisions, we can make better ones? Because don't we all want better for our kids than we do for ourselves? My parents did, and maybe that's where I got a lot of strength, or it could have been the fact that I was the youngest in the family and I couldn't stand what I saw when people took advantage of others. I saw my mom, dad, and brother just stand back and watch while I jumped in and ran with a task, they didn't even tackle. Sometimes it wasn't the greatest decision that I ever made (even to this day), but at least I didn't stand around and watch—this is what I am most proud of in my life.

As I sit here thinking, I am reminded by the date. It's mid-July 2010, and school will start soon. My son will be starting 9th grade this year. My, how the times have changed. I remember when I was pregnant with him and our main priority was to build my ex's "dream house." He seemed to work on it a lot and was never around. I know his priority was for all of us to be a family in our new own home. Even though I was the one who cleaned it, did the laundry and took care of our son during those five years of living there, I do give him credit for building an awesome house. But, with my commute it was hardly worth it sometimes. I was so tired most of the time that it was hard to enjoy it. The over 100 miles a day on the road with a baby was hard on me. My weight was up and I'm sure it was a contributing factor for my high blood pressure.

So, I guess when divorce happens, everyone looks back and tries to explain why things happened as they did. Do we silently want to have a "go back" experience so we can have a "re-do?" Or would we go back and tell that SOB to take a long hike off a short pier? Possibly. But isn't that something that everyone would do if they could? I know there are a lot of things I'd like to take back or not even do if I could. But where would I be today if I did that? I probably wouldn't have my son, and I may not be living where I am today without those experiences. I could have even married another idiot and had gone through the same thing. So, I guess, there's some reasons a person has to tip toe through the quicksand to get to the other side.

I guess in a way I was lucky, yes lucky, that I didn't spend all my life with this man and took the abuse that I did take. He wanted to move on and even though I got very angry and upset with his actions, he has now released me from my chains. I guess I could have been involved with a man who was out to ruin my credit, take whatever money I had, and make me a bigger fool than I feel right now, but he didn't. At least that's one good thing that came out of this whole debacle.

The weekend is upon me again and the weather is heating up. The forecast says 100 degrees tomorrow, but I guess it's expected. It is July after all. So, what was I doing last year at this time? I don't know, but I'm sure I was still in shock. A month has passed at this time, and I'm not sure what I was feeling. Today it's a little different, even though several months had lapsed. I don't think I'm still numb, but some of the same feelings are still there. However, as each day passes, I gain a little more independence—I think. I'm not sure if my confidence will ever fully come back. It's like on that same damn roller coaster and I have no control. I'm not even sure if meeting and then dating a new "prospect" will even get my self-assurance to return. Do I need to be the one who must be stronger than ever before? Besides, what am I trying to prove at this point in my life? We are all out to get ahead of the pact, and the things we are challenged with down that "yellow brick road" are the things that will define our character. Either we avoid those objects, or we zap them with our radar gun, destroy them, and venture forward. I think I just need more Mountain Dew to get that caffeine buzz going in my body.

Today is Saturday and I got roped into taking my son to a bicycle competition. As I waited for each of the age groups to race, I laid on the ground soaking up the sun's rays. All around me were families whose children were in the competition. I don't know what it was, but I kept hearing children laughing and playing and saying "daddy." Those words really seemed to haunt me somehow. There I was in the middle of an event filled with "happy" couples with children—once again. There were fathers caring for their sons and daughters, and husbands having conversations with their buddies about their wives. The conversations were cordial and loving. The only argument I heard was the one with a couple's daughter who wanted to ride her bike without a helmet. There were no disagreements between husbands and wives—only conversations regarding the events of the day. Once again, I felt alone in a crowd. Maybe I didn't fit in once more? Have I ever fit in anywhere? I'm still trying to figure out that one. I don't even know why I keep having this conversation with myself—again!

I guess this past year has been such a struggle for me and it continues to be a struggle. Plus, I'm sure that everyone going through a divorce has been at a crossroads—just like me. Whether or not their ex cheated on them, or just left them in the lurch is where "that" question still does not come easy for me. Why must good people go through so many bad events in their lives? Are we all in line for our halos that will appear sometime in our future? Are we supposed to just choke down all the bad stuff in our lives to get to the good? I just want to find the answers before I give up on something ever happening that will make me feel like I've finally arrived at the finish line. I'm ready for that point in my life.

Looking back at my life from its earliest point I remember so many good and bad things—maybe too well. From my alcoholic father to my first date, I remember praying to keep the focus that I needed to get through each event. In addition, it sometimes didn't feel as if God heard my voice as I cried, because I was so depressed as a teenager. I tried not to let anyone know, but I'm not sure if I succeeded. However, I'm sure God was there—somewhere. Were things I wanted to accomplish just out of my reach because I couldn't touch them? Maybe I needed more wisdom to understand how things worked back then. If I had had more knowledge, perhaps I could have made more of an impact in my life and in the lives of others. Today, years later, I am still trying to find that understanding in my heart to go forth and prosper.

I am finding that people who are sad seem to doubt themselves—and sometimes a lot. Hesitation and uncertainty are also present, and it seems to be the first thing we feel when divorce is staring at us in the face. I am still wondering how to erase those thoughts and feelings after almost a year later. In addition to feeling this way, how do we make our children feel ok about what has happened or will happen? Plus, how do we explain to them what their future holds because mom and dad aren't together anymore? How do we meet their needs—still—and know when to change for the better? When do we get our confidence back, so we stop doubting our actions? I do know that we need to pray for our children's future so that they will gain the confidence and obtain the direction they need to grow up in this messed-up world. I guess we need to hope that our children acquire the spiritual guidance that only God can give. I suppose we can build anything with the right tools because our children should be our priority.

Ok, I guess we're at the point to speak about Pity Parties, right? We've all been there. Sometimes we even stay longer than we want. But where does it get us? Nowhere, right? Doesn't God want to us do great things in our life? Well, that's a definite no brainer! Of course he does. Why would he want us to fall flat on our face, and then give up? I know we all have those thoughts. There's no way to always be happy or to just be totally miserable all the time. Just remember, when you are at your weakest, you can also be at your strongest. I know I can't make it on my own. A higher power is there to help me; I just know it. God will help me as well as others in this same circumstance and give us what we need to move forward and succeed.

It's Monday once more. As I look back, I remember not too long ago each day had a number nearing the one-year mark and each day was much more of a challenge. My job in Human Services is even challenging. There are a lot of people that I deal with who are at their lowest point in their lives. After a while their sad stories get to you. It doesn't help if you're at your lowest point too. Keeping your focus and wanting to cheerfully go on is such a challenge some days. I want so much to be happy once again, but when will it come? At this point in my life, I really do not want to believe that divorce has ruined me; nor has it destroyed my destiny. I am a "good" person; I deserve the best that life can give, right? Not just for me, but everyone who feels like life will never get better for them must realize that bad times are only one part of your life. It is a challenge—of course—but the bad times are only a part of what we deal with. The good times will come again, too! I hope.

There's got to be a silver lining out there for everyone who is depressed since his or her marriage didn't work out. In addition, it always seems that divorce always brings so much crap that it's hard to concentrate. Every little thing that happens in their situation creates more and more depression. How can you hold your head up when you know that at every turn, you can stumble once again? Just remember, that's why God allowed man to build a crutch, and if that doesn't work, God will carry you on a stretcher—designed just for you!

Well, when you think things are going ok, well guess what? Here's a new challenge—I think I have hit a new low when it comes to relationships. A guy I dated late last year called me up and wanted "one last time with me." What the Hell does that mean? Am I now a professional call girl, and should he leave money by the bedside? I wasn't sure if I should be offended or if I should be flattered. He obviously still feels something for me, but what a way to show it! Now, I know what you're thinking. Did she or didn't she go to his house for that last cocktail? Well, ladies and gentlemen, I told him very politely that it wasn't a good idea. I am not going to lower my principles in that way. I guess it's like what I've been saying all along, dating after divorce is a pain in the keester!

I guess I don't understand men at all. Right when I think I know what they want, they turn around and totally floor me. This person, who came into my life not so long ago, really made me think that I had met my soul mate. However, he has run away from me several times. He has that need to be near someone, but once he gets close, something spooks him, and he runs like a scared rabbit. I just know he hasn't dealt with his past, and I can't help him because he doesn't want help. I am so fed up with his actions, too, that I'm at that "done" point in my life with him. I just want to be with someone who wants to be with me, and not give me conditions on a relationship. Maybe that's the way we should all look at relationships. We should feel comfortable with that person, share the good and bad times, and lean on each other when needed. Why should one person dominate a relationship? Well, duh! When I look back, I wonder what happened to my thinking since I "let" my ex-husband control most of my actions. Do we just want to please that person in some way? Or do we just want a relationship to work, and will we do anything to make that happen? Well, I did it, and I'm almost ashamed to admit it. Plus, I'm sure there are men and women out there who have done the same, but they can't admit it!

Every relationship has a way of teaching us new goals and ambitions in our life. But after a divorce, those expectations can be skewed a little. Our confusion still lingers, but we now know we don't want to have a relationship like the one we just left. However, I've seen women and men go right back into a bond with someone who was just like the one they left. Is it a fact that we do this because it is familiar, or because we just can't break free of what we once knew? I mean, look at me, I left a relationship where my ex was very controlling, and the two men I have dated since seem to have a little bit of a control issue too. Fortunately for me, I singled this out quickly as something I need to watch out for, and to not fall for it once again. If a relationship were to work out for me with someone, I guess I need for their control to subside and their guard needs to come down off that throne of power.

Life seems to throw those lessons out there just as fast as you can either dodge them or catch and throw them back. Every day seems like a new challenge and dealing with more and more issues is irritating, but it's not as bad as dealing with my divorce last year. For example, I am still having warranty issues with my townhouse, but I feel like I'm still in charge somehow. It sounds strange, but now I make decisions and making people conform is what I have control over. However, it doesn't happen as quickly as I wish it could. I guess there's always going to be something going on that irritates me; but it's the way you control your actions that has you in turmoil or in limbo or even going down the right path—am I right? So, how do we get to this point in our lives? One way I guess is to pray and not lose your heart in the process. Be always ready for that next crisis and plan how to handle it—easier said than done, I guess, huh? With crises comes that feeling of being overwhelmed and sometimes we don't speak up for ourselves. Sometimes we just want to give up and not go on, but we must. If we have kids in the mix, they see our actions and we can't let them down—not now, not ever! For, our actions speak louder than words. "Monkey See, Monkey Do" is the saying that now comes to mind. Plus, how do we feel when we think our prayers are not answered right away? The first thing in my mind is that God doesn't hear me, or he doesn't exist. However, I know he does exist. For example, I have a habit of losing my keys if they are not in the right spot. All I do is to say, "God, I need a little help here, can you help me find them?" I'm telling you, within five minutes or less, I will find those dang keys! Sounds rather silly, but it does work. Right when I get frustrated, he helps me find something like my keys. I also have found that when I've needed directions lately, he's there. I'm not sure where he's leading me to until I show up at that location, but I do get an answer. I guess we should never give up because we all need guidance and support from those everyday things that happen that we do and do not have control over in our lives.

There are a few things that prayer gives us—such as it brings us back to a biblical perspective. I guess it's like saying or even asking what God would do in this situation that we are currently involved in now. Prayer can also give us faith and courage in the rough times. It lifts our head when we are discouraged, and it can restore peace and quiet to our lives. I know it has given me more than I've asked for lately, and it's been a good thing. I don't feel as worried and lost as I once did a year ago. Whenever I've gotten to another low point in my thinking, all I do is look to the man upstairs and ask for help and a path. My strength has been renewed since last year at this time. I know I can accomplish what I set out for, and with a hand to guide me; I know it will come true.

13th Chapter

Go Forth and Conquer

My year of "almost complete freedom" is almost up. It is now the last week of July. There are only two more months until that fateful day in September of last year. You know that day when my ex and I walked into the courtroom separately, but walked out together? I still look back and wonder what led us to this point. All those memories with the good and bad times were attached to my hip. Should we both have done things differently? Well, that's a no-brainer! In some ways, it's like we didn't try hard enough to stay married. In other ways, we were both selfish—maybe him more than me, but that's of course my opinion! Somewhere down that path we parted ways and never came together again, and the scariest thing is that we never wanted to go back.

So, are we both happier now? I'm sure there are times when we both wonder what would have happened if we were still a team. I guess it's interesting to think about those "what ifs'" in life. I'm sure if we all had an opportunity to go back in time and change something in our lives, we would. Just think of all those missed opportunities such as lost loves and job opportunities that we wished we could have now. But do we really miss those things in our life? Everyone grows just a little when we have failures in life. If everything always went precisely as we wished, we'd never learn anything, right? We would never appreciate what we now have—even though we whine about what we do have. Think about it. If God gave us everything we ever wanted, we'd be the biggest bunch of spoiled brats in the world! I'm right—you know I am!

So, what do we want when we don't know what we want? That seems to be the ultimate question when we are in unfamiliar territory, huh? I guess the short answer is to focus, get a direction, and go down that straight path. Ha! Who the Hell thought of that one? That straight path seems to be filled with lots of potholes and detours if you ask me. Nothing is guaranteed in this world, but I guess it's the way you look at life and what you want that will move you in a certain direction. If you complain about what you don't have, but don't do anything to change it, get a grip! Remember the definition of insanity is doing something the same way over and over and expecting a different result. Hello? Are you there? If these words make you mad, it should. So, go out there and conquer those things you've always wanted to do. So, you need to quit complaining about the life you don't have and not making changes to fix it. Ok? I know it's hard; believe me, I'm there now. Every day is a challenge for me, and I never know what is around the corner, but I have to deal with what comes my way and eliminate the things that I don't want to exist in my life. Remember, things will occur in our lives; it's just the way we allow it to affect us that either makes or breaks us. I guess it could be compared to military boot camp, games are played, but it's how we show our emotions that will either guarantee our victory or make us the weak link in game of life.

Just think, our thoughts can take us to places we've never imagined. So, why do we allow ourselves to sometimes go down a path of destruction? Can we ever recover and quit beating ourselves up over our judgments? Some people have no feelings and don't realize what they have created within themselves and for others around them. On the flip side, some people regurgitate those thoughts brought on by others and themselves. I must admit—that's me! Do I over think everything that is said by others? Sometimes. Maybe it's the something that my mom told me when I was young; she would say that I should be ashamed of myself when I did something she thought wasn't right. Maybe it stuck with me too much. Perhaps it sunk deep into my soul and festered, becoming more and more uncomfortable to destroy my being.

As I sit here at my kitchen table, I am constantly reminded how my thoughts have changed my life. The townhouses being built just behind mine are just about completed. The drywall is in each unit, the kitchen cabinets are going in, the hot water heaters and furnaces are also being delivered today. There is a big truck parked in front with bathtubs, sinks and hoses all being delivered this morning. Soon, the units will be done, and I'll have new neighbors. Will they restart their lives—just like I did? They'll be in a new environment, just like I chose my life to be. Or is their newly married or newly divorced life one that will change them and their goals?

Well, I have found out that there is at least one female moving in who is getting divorced. What is it about living in a townhouse environment that seems to draw divorcees? I mean, in just two buildings, there are four of us who are divorced—now we are adding another person to our club.

Does she even know that our "club" exists? Probably not, but she will soon. Can you say, "divorcee block party?"

I guess with all the new neighbors there will be a lot more kids around here. Thus far, there have been a few little ones around, but not many. Soon there will be more teenagers too; I'm not sure if that will be a problem or not. School is also around the corner. Now another year is starting for my son. One more year will be going by and only too quickly. I remember last year when I had to tell his school what had happened, and I asked them to be sensitive to his needs. His feelings were all over the board and I wasn't sure how to handle it. Here was just one more thing to deal with without "that" handbook. It's funny how life's curveballs just come at you one right after the other, and you're not sure if you should dodge them or catch them and throw them back. I just hope that I can survive through this game called life until my son becomes an adult.

The next stage of a person's life or a "divorcee's" life is one that seems to be scrutinized—a lot sometimes. Have we failed in some way and are we now considered "rejects" in some way because we failed at marriage? I remember a long time ago when I dated a guy who was divorced with two children. My dad didn't like him because he considered him a "reject." If my father were still alive today, would he think that of me in that way? Would he feel that I botched my marriage in some way to where I couldn't keep my man? Have I failed in his eyes? Those questions are quite complicated and for some reason, I don't think these thoughts would cross his mind. But I'm almost certain that my dad would have stood behind me always—he would be my biggest fan.

I believe there is a bond between you and your parents, and they would help you stay with you in any way if they supported you. I feel the same way with my friends—they will have your back when you can't straighten it, and they will pick you up when you fall. I guess my advice is to select your friends very carefully because they can be your strength—sometimes more than your family when they are not available. Don't get wrong me wrong, my family is there for me; they're just over a thousand miles east. I have all their emotional support they can muster and I'm thankful they are available, even though they're a telephone call away.

So, in this new life of mine, how do I understand what my destiny has planned for me? What is God's Will now? Do I have a new purpose and what is it composed of? In church this morning, I may have gotten my answer. The Pastor spoke of three things that a person needs to have to make sure they are on their right path. One must have a desire, peace of mind, and an open door. You must have all three, or the decision you are in the process of making won't conform to your direction. This really makes sense. Think about that new adventure you want. If it takes you away from your family and your faith for more hours than you used to, it's probably not the right move. If you don't feel peaceful about it, maybe you can't live with yourself. For example, the first townhouse I put an offer on was a little more than what I wanted to pay, and I wasn't comfortable paying any more. I guess there was a reason why I didn't get it. Besides, I didn't really get bummed about the fact that I didn't get it. The peace I feel about the place I'm in now is real and I know it was meant to be.

I guess the next question to ask yourself is, "Are you in a situation where you will grow with God?" Now you're asking yourself, "What?" Before this morning, I had no answer to this either. But my understanding is that we must be comfortable in our own skin. If we don't like our situation, ask for guidance (from the one above), give thanks for the little things, and always be grateful for what you have. At this point you probably still have no clue what that is, but that's when you ask for help.

As for me, I'm still wondering if what I'm doing is making any sense, and if I'm on that correct path. Am I hearing the answers I need from that man upstairs to survive? I certainly hope so at this point, because, that next relationship must be one that works equally between us. Think of a connection this way—for it to work, it must be sacrificial and unconditional by each person. Our spouse, or significant other, must love us as they love themselves, right? For, if this doesn't happen, each person could go off in his or her own direction—and separately. Conceit and self-centeredness aren't what any relationship can conform to—let alone survive. I have no desire to do that crap again! Besides it sounds little crazy, and I'm a little bit of a feminist, so when the Bible says that the man is the head of the household, I'm a little skeptical. But as you read that passage, this is where it says that each person should cling to each other and basically hold each one in the highest regard. Sounds hard to do if a person is stuck on himself or herself and doesn't care enough about the special person in his life, right?

I guess it's what a person really wants out of life and how far they will go to make a relationship work. Think of it this way, a person can have spots and wrinkles. God can wash away the spots and smooth out the wrinkles, but only if this person asks for the help. Makes sense to me! Plus, if husbands loved their wives as they loved themselves, and vice versa, we'd have a perfect world, right? Who knows? On the flip side, if we would only love our neighbor's half as much as we loved ourselves, we'd be living in a different world. Once again, it's a lifestyle we agree to live—or not to live.

Marital relationships are ones in which we either feel we've won or lost. When we divorce, we feel like we've stumbled hard, and if it happens more than once, we have that shame pointing us towards failure once more in our lives. Then, at least once a year, that "Divorce" anniversary comes back to haunt us. Will we ever get to the point where we will forget that day? I certainly hope so at this point of my life. I know I am regretting that fateful anniversary. It's just around the corner, and it will be here before I know it.

So, weren't we taught that a man shall leave his mother and father and cling to his wife to become "one?" That's what the Bible says, but what does that really mean and where is that dang handbook on the subject when I need it? I guess it's sort of like having a baby, there's no child-rearing book that completely works there either. So, the only other thing that I really see is that men and women both need to be respected and loved. Am I right? Does this make any sense? I really think it does. Men sometimes have that "macho" attitude, and if their wife disrespects them in front of friends and family, they're now not a "man" anymore. If a woman doesn't feel like she's loved, she'll retreat somehow and find that love she so desperately needs. It may not be with her husband, either. For, something dies inside a person when they are disrespected or unloved. I guess emotionally we need that awesome feeling that puts us upon a pedestal by the one who loves us—well, it sounds good anyway. I just know that when I was married, I didn't feel loved, and I felt very disrespected by my ex. In turn, I'm sure I disrespected him to a certain point because of how I felt. I guess I didn't want to put in the effort for him to feel good, when he wouldn't reciprocate the same to me.

Somewhere down that road to "happily ever after," we saw Adam and Eve make the wrong decisions in their relationship. It was the same for my ex and me. He saw the green grass on the other side of the fence, and he wanted to go over there instead of watering our side to make it flourish once again. But, dwelling on what could have been, is not where I want to be anymore. Remember, to live is to awaken from that slumber we call divorce. To die is to let our failures control our being. So, don't go there—ever—just have one thought that will take you to where you know you should be. So, what is that thought? It's different for everyone, and I'm not the one to tell you where you should be at this point in your life. It's the vision you have for yourself and where you want to be in six months, one year, and five years down that road we call life. So, get a plan straight in your head, and then put it down on paper to point you to that straight and narrow path. It can't begin until you put your mind to it.

Remember, your life cannot "commence" until you're at that "done" point in your life. So, what are you waiting for? Get your pen and paper and write those words you so desperately want off your tongue. Say them aloud and to your friends. You know you want to do this, so quit hesitating and do it now!

Time seems to pass so quickly sometimes. For instance, I checked the last horrid e-mail that my ex and I had sent to each other, it was almost two months ago! Wow, all that energy we spent yelling at each other and about what? I guess everything he did to me for those years came out in those e-mails. My voice became apparent to everyone and especially my ex. Everything he did made my skin crawl, and his decisions helped get us to where we both are now. Maybe I am upset that he changed my life forever because his choices affected me without my permission. Was it that I wanted to work on our relationship—no, not really. He made me sad and lonely for a long time. I'm just glad that I was the one who busted him—it was quite a rush of energy because for once I was in control. Did he really do me a favor by doing his dirty deed? Well, that's a "no brainer"! Yes!

I was even reminded this morning that if a man cheats on his spouse, he is a scumbag. While listening to the radio, I heard a conversation between a woman and the DJs. She was telling them that her husband had left her after one year of marriage, and then sent pictures of him and the new chick having relations. What the @!X%*? She was obviously devastated, and words of encouragement flowed from the DJs on the radio. I've heard of some idiots in my time, but really! Well, they kept telling her that she was better off without that idiot, but did she really hear those words? I also think that's the way I felt; I knew he was cheating, and when I finally confronted him, he did come clean. So, wouldn't it be easier if one just left instead of putting on a façade of marriage? If you're that unhappy, either work on that relationship or leave! Sounds easy, huh? Unfortunately, it sometimes doesn't work that way. It seems we're stuck in a rut and a four-wheel drive can't get us out of that ditch. It seems when we fall apart; we can't breathe and then we freeze in time. We try to hold onto that person for as long as we can, and not let go—either physically or emotionally. Why? I wish I knew, for I felt as if I wasted almost 19 years of my life when I could have been happy with my real soul mate. However, we can't hold onto that guilt, frustration, or whatever you want to call it, or we will lose the game of life!

Looking back, we can't beat ourselves up too badly about a relationship that has crashed and burned, or we'd lose whatever sanity we once had. I'm right; you know it! I guess it's a little different when it's a dating relationship versus a marriage. There's just more on the line to fail. If you have kids, assets, and a home together, it seems harder to let go. The baggage seems to follow you around for longer than you want. Especially if one person has an affair; it really weighs heavy on your heart. I know I've had to deal with my feelings in a way I've never done before. Dating used to be a lot easier before I got married. When I'd break up with a guy, there were no major issues to deal with. I'd go for a drive, drink a little too much, and then cry on a friend's shoulder. But I'd get over it and move on rather quickly. Now, it's all different. Now, my immediate needs and wants, my son, in addition to my retirement years are involved. Will I ever grow old with someone who will always be glad to see me first thing in the morning? Will I smile when I get a call from that special someone? Then, will they want to grow old with me and be my constant companion? Several questions I guess will always linger in my mind. I don't know where I am going from here; I guess I must enjoy the ride?

As I look out my window today, I see a concrete truck pouring the driveways of the units just behind my townhouse. Soon, the dirt will be a silent memory, and in just a few short weeks I will have new neighbors. I have watched the construction workers go from flat ground to now another building, which will house families of all sorts. As the world keeps turning, and so do the lives of everyone around me—

to include myself. I am at a loss sometimes because nothing stands still. I don't think it ever did. With loss, destruction, as well as divorce, everything keeps moving at a pace unlike my own.

Sometimes I guess we think that everything should stop when we are devastated. I can compare this to watching an accident unfold. Everything seems to go in slow motion, and then a crash happens. Once, I saw a car go too fast in a turn lane during a snowstorm, and it went straight into a light pole instead of turning right. In dry weather, they would have been fine. It was just that a "snowstorm" caught them off guard. I guess it's strange to compare the two, but it always seems that one event changes a couple's direction; especially if that union has issues in the first place.

Getting back into a church setting has really helped me heal over the past year. Today, nevertheless, I was not disappointed. The words I heard today really made me think. They were, "If you change your mind, God can change your heart." This made so much sense to me, and it really makes me see how one's significant other thinks when they want to cheat. If you're not ready to see that special person in your life as an equal; your heart will never change your mind. Ok, think of it this way, and it's only my opinion, your significant other can hold himself or herself to a higher esteem and others around them don't count. In addition, if they're not ready to see you as an equal guess what, you're not. Are they trying to be better than their significant other? Or do they undergo a series of feelings, emotions, and whatever else is more important than that person to which they said, "I Do?" From examining my friends and co-workers who have gone through a divorce, this is what I have concluded. So, what happened to holding your spouse to the same level as yourself? Why must one person be more important than the other in a relationship?

I think that's where my ex and I went wrong. I did too much for him from the beginning when we first dated, and then throughout our marriage he expected it. This made our relationship so imbalanced that it was impossible for me to escape. I felt trapped for so long, while he had a good time being well cared for. For so long, I didn't feel important, equal, nor did I feel his respect. Sad, huh? This didn't happen overnight. It was years of abuse that snuck up on me and bit me on my backside, and the sad part is I let it happen. I was so miserable that nothing else mattered but to try to exist. Now, I see my ex driving a BMW SUV that his girlfriend bought, and my son is saying that his dad is acting like he's "hot stuff." What happened? I guess he's still at that point of putting himself higher than others. It's almost as if he's trying to be at a higher position so he can be in control of someone or something in his life once again. I just want to know one thing, when did he get to the point that he has to be "somebody" to exist? I've known people like this in my life, and each person went through something traumatic in their childhoods. Now as adults they need to prove something—like they matter, and they are above those happenings years ago. It's a shame they cannot look back and grow from that horrible experience instead of using others for their advantage in life.

I guess it's how you view life in general when you're a child that will make or break you as an adult. Think about it. If tragedy, in your eyes, happens all around you and you can't think rationally, what tools are you given to cope? I saw my dad do some things when I was in elementary school that still haunts me to this day. So, what have I done about them?

I have learned from those experiences and relate them to my everyday life now. I realize that others can go through tragedy just as I did and now, I can feel for them—I don't want to be above them in some way. Sure, I want to live comfortably, but it won't be at the expense of others in my life. First and foremost, I give myself to my religion, then unto the people in my life. I guess some people are just out to get what they can from others and go on—my guilt won't let me do that. Don't get me wrong, I make mistakes too, and on that note, I try to treat people like I would like to be treated. Isn't that the way we should live? I guess if we did, life would be a whole lot better, right?

That year mark is creeping up on me faster than I realized. My son has reminded me of that fact, since my birthday is just around the corner. I can remember last year how difficult it was without my ex being at the dinner table with me. I specifically remember that it would be different from now on, and specifically, if my ex's mother felt obliged to join us for my birthday dinner. I was surprised that she did join my son and me, and it felt strange. I knew my life had really fallen apart and where I took it from here, would define my direction. All the events that have passed me by in these months would either make me a normal person again or I would lose all my sanity. So many times, I was at the breaking point, but somehow, I stayed on the straight and narrow path. I guess the question I need to ask myself now is will I get passed my birthday, and that eventful date—just 21 days after my birthday?

Well, September 22 is coming fast, and it will be here before I know it. At this point, how will I feel? Will it be another starting point in my life? Or will the sadness consume me as it did last year? Those "walking papers" are worth a lot, or are they? I guess the anniversary of anything can be devastating or a very happy occasion. Almost 10 years ago, my dad died from a heart attack on December 22. Each year afterwards, it didn't get any easier. I cried at songs that reminded me of him, but I just tried to get through the day as best as I could. But, with any occasion, certain people can bring up ideas that will make our psyche return to those bad times too, but we can't go there, or at least not stay there for too long.

Even though anniversaries are memorable, speaking with our ex's can also be memorable. Today, I talked via e-mail to him. We had a pleasant conversation—hold me upright; I'm about to faint! We talked only about our son and kept it as cordial as possible. I hadn't talked to him in almost two months, and after those exchanges, I didn't want to repeat them. Wow! What happened to us? It felt strange; needless to say, everything feels weird lately. Now, I guess I should ask myself when did the waters part to allow us to walk across the riverbed together as "friends"? Well, maybe we shouldn't be friends quite yet. I guess things can calm down, but it could also be that our different directions are finally far enough apart that we don't have to touch each other.

At this point in my "divorce career," I have made new friends, joined a couple of singles groups, and decided that this divorce was the best thing that ever happened to me. I'm even seeing others around me who divorced last year going in their own direction. One co-worker whom I thought got married too quickly after her divorce is already having marital problems. Can we all love past our pain so we can get to a "happily ever after?" Does it really exist? Are we destined to be with our true soul mate? I really feel that we must overcome our fears and hurt and then, maybe, we can let that love, we truly need, to enter into our heart.

I guess you could compare love to an addiction. We all want it, but how we control it will be the true test of our being. I guess it's like being two-years old, there's a lot of energy in one body. We just must know how to put it to good use, so that it's not out of control. We must also choose that special someone who will be there for us for good and bad times. They cannot constantly have excuses to not want to be with us. Work cannot control them; they must know when to quit working and know when to play. There must also be a balance, for if something shifts, the control we have on our lives will be also shifted.

It has almost been a year, and I still feel confused. I still don't have a clue how my life will end up, but I know each day is getting me closer to my destiny. I so much want a love I so deserve. I can't judge other men as the one who just left. I just need to weigh my options and figure out if they really want to commit to me, and fully! I want to be with someone who will take time for me and be there for me, and I am there for him. So far, I don't think I've found that special someone. I thought I had twice now, but I don't think either one of them were at the same point as me in life to share everything. Is any man in my future there to mess up things just because he is scared to feel a real love? I feel sad for anyone who can't find his or her true soul mate. However, I cannot quit trying to find "him." I would not be giving myself justice if I let a coward change me and not move forward.

Just remember, if you get the opportunity to "repay" someone for the pain they cause you, and you don't, I guess you're over it. You may not be over the pain, but you've moved one step closer to resolution. I guess this is what we all must think about when it's really time to go forth and conquer our fears towards our love life. No one said it would be easy, but we must evaluate what we want in life, and the path we take to get there. Should we reflect backwards to those times that we shared, with that ex of ours, so that we won't repeat those times in the future? Do we now watch movies with a happy ending and wish we were in their shoes? Or do we watch movies that make us realize that we are not the only people on the earth who are dealing with cheating spouses? This weekend I watched, "Diary of a Mad Black Woman," and "Why Did I Get Married?" In both movies, there are real-life choices that make us cry, laugh, and wonder what the future will hold. They also make us wonder what we did in our relationship that our ex would betray us in this way. The questions we ask ourselves when we feel so low are ones we need to revisit, but not obsess about. I have watched these movies before, and each time the feelings of hurt and anger are still present. What a rush!

Feeling like we've lost it all in a relationship is probably one of the first things that goes through us like a lightening bolt. Perhaps we think God isn't there when our tragedy hits, but he had a plan for each one of us. He took me out of a bad marriage that didn't work and gave me the freedom I so desperately needed. My ex, along with God, gave me the power to smile again. They both took away my agony and gave me a reason to live. God got me to this point so I could get my life back on track and to view myself differently. I was created for a purpose and a plan. I wasn't put here on this earth to be miserable—I totally believe that. Strained relationships and marriages sometimes can't be saved. I guess it depends on the circumstances, so when a disaster hits, God is always there to show that he is in control and to hold things together. We may not feel that he is there but believe he is there!

Our faith is always tested when a catastrophe hits, and it is always based on evidence of things we can't see. It's like what's behind the curtain at a play. Each time it shuts, we believe that the next scene will be present when that curtain is opened once again. It's as if God is preparing the stage for the next event in my life. I know I need to respond to my faith for it will evolve into what I was meant to be.

14th Chapter

One Year Later

At this point in my story, I thought I was out of words, but after waking up at 3am this morning, I was wrong. I lay in bed for about 30 minutes, and then I turned on the TV and started watching a movie. It immediately caught my attention because it was about a battered wife. She stayed with her husband even after he hit her constantly, and on a few occasions, he put her in the hospital. It was only after her son started displaying the same traits that she finally realized that she had to leave. Maybe I thought I was over those feelings when my ex yelled at me time and time again, and then put me down. Wrong! Those same sick thoughts of helplessness came over me and made me relive all those feelings of last year. I knew where she came from. I knew how helpless she felt, and it wasn't a pleasant feeling. I just wanted to turn off the program and go back to sleep. I eventually did, but, Wow! I was floored to believe that I haven't gotten over that way of thinking about the hurt and despair that is obviously still hidden away-way behind my heart.

I don't understand. He's out of my life—sort of—but I can't move on. Why? What happened to that strong woman I knew 20 years ago who didn't put up with any kind of crap? Was I beaten down that bad that I still, after almost a year, cannot regroup? Now, my son is having flashbacks from the other house. Since I did a little painting in my new place, his anger issues are coming back. He doesn't want me to change anything once again. I think that this anniversary is affecting him too. I tried to talk to him and tell him that I am here whenever he wanted to talk—even if he wanted to call me from his dad's place. I don't think he will, but the offer is out there, and I am trying to get him to think rationally about this whole mess. The way we think can keep us imprisoned in our mind—but only if we let it. On that note, there's an excerpt from the Bible that I am reminded of—it's in 2 Corinthians 10, and it states, "We can either take our thoughts captive or allow them to take us captive." I guess that saying is easier said than done, but I know letting out your thoughts is the first step to healing your heart and mind.

So, does healing have a way of making you think you're cured! Ha! I probably should beat myself for saying those words. For instance, I recently had a co-worker tell me that when your significant other wants to spend time by themselves, they're up to something! In my case, it was true. So, that question keeps arising every time I have trust issues of this past year. Where are those guys I've seen when I can't get in touch with them? Are they doing something they shouldn't be, or do they think I'm doing the same thing? How will I ever trust anyone—especially a man, again? It seems like past experiences really can hit home when it comes to future events. Besides, where is that trust gene I once knew, and how do I get it back since it "left" me? Did it run and hide for good, and will it ever come out to play "nice" again? Will my old emotions let me be the same—ever? I think that the same hurt will always be there somewhere lurking around the corner in that forbidden closet. Then, someone will open that door again by accident, or on purpose, and I'm right back to Day One of busting apart another relationship. There again I will feel that same hurt all over again; I'm not sure it's even worth it a second time! The next occasion may be the same scenario of a significant other cheating on me again, or not. God, help me to trust again, because I'm not into this "hurt" game anymore. No wonder my mother stayed single after my dad died. She didn't want to re-live those same experiences even one more time. We recently asked each other if either of us had found a man yet. After we both said, "No," we just laughed. It seemed strange that we had this conversation, but we did. I just knew at that moment; I never want to get married again. Sure, I may change my mind in the future, but right now, I'm just not going that direction. For, I won't just settle for someone this time—just to have a companion and to please my mother. I'd rather die first than be with a man who makes me miserable.

I once saw a Maxine cartoon that said, "Sure marriage can be fun some of the time. Trouble is, you're married all the time." Another cartoon from Maxine said this, "A man without a woman is a bachelor. A woman without a man is a genius." Some days I look at these sayings and laugh, but other days I totally agree with them. I guess my anger is still there—you know, down deep within my heart, and it has yet to heal.

There are new things constantly happening all around me, and getting used to it is sometimes a challenge. Once again, I am sitting at my kitchen table watching the final construction of that building. I have watched it being built for months now, and its completion is just around the corner. Where will the new families come from and what baggage will they carry with them? This baggage doesn't constitute leather bags; it will be their past and it may not be pretty. They, like me, want to begin a new existence—on a solid foundation free of what they want to forget or with whom they want to start anew.

Each time I see a good relationship, I guess I'm still flabbergasted that they still exist. For example, at noon today, I noticed a co-worker whose husband came to meet her for lunch. As he approached her, a faint smile came upon his face as well as hers. They had originally met on an online dating service last year, dated for five months, was engaged at 10 months, and then married. What a whirlwind romance! They had both been divorced for years and had dated other people for a long time before they met. Each relationship they both had, well, it never lasted until now. Somehow, someway, they clicked as a pair and now they are joined together as a married couple. They were obviously meant to be together, and I applaud them for their commitment. Shouldn't all relationships be that way?

As we look at our relations in life, we must also consider the one we have with God. Are we faithful to him as we would be with our soul mate? If the answer is "No," then we are cheating ourselves along with our faith. Are we worshiping such things as money, fame, and power to the highest degree possible? If the answer is yes, then I think we must re-examine our life goals. Are these things that will someday make us happy—truly happy in life? I guess if we don't function to the capacity that the "higher one" wants us to, then we're not growing and learning from our past mistakes, relationships, or whatever we're currently going through.

We've been placed on this earth to do what we're meant to do, so how does this relate to our significant other and ourselves? I only know that we need to be true to ourselves, and to put our relationships in the highest regard just as our higher power. We need to seek out those gaps and weaknesses that we have in addition to those insecurities that affect us. We can't allow our minds to seek the things that destroy our wants. I guess what I'm saying is that valuing that special someone in one's life is a task worth taking on, for each person deserves that special love.

I truly believe that taking advantage of that special person in your life is not acceptable behavior. If this is how one feels; well, they aren't your soul mate, right? If you want out—well, then, get out! Making them feel like the "fool" is no way for anyone to act, nor feel. Believe me, I've been feeling it all year. The strange thing is that the anniversary of my divorce is in 31 days. Plus, it's August 22, 2010, and in just over a week, it will be my birthday and I, again, will celebrate it without "him." I even had a conversation with a friend of which I told them it still feels weird to live by myself—even after all this time. If this wasn't enough, I found out that a relative who got divorced just one month before me last year is now engaged again—and to a guy with the same first name as her ex! Yikes!! When I said this to a friend, she said, "What is she thinking?" As for me, I'm not sure what to think now, nor can I trust my feelings. Am I wiser than I was just a few months ago? At this point in time, who knows? I guess it's just hard to know where to go next.

So, where will I be next year, in five years, or even 10 years down the line? Will I ever trust enough again to remarry? Besides, look at all those couples that have taken the plunge again to say, "I Do." Did they ever revisit those old emotions, but somehow this time is different? I would like to know their secrets to happiness, for it seems it will be a long time before I can really go there once again. I guess now I just need the strength to get to that point because where my head goes, so will my body, right?

That mind/body thing still gets to me. For example, last night I had a dream that I got engaged to a guy. What? Perhaps I was thinking too much about my relative getting engaged so soon after her divorce. Maybe it's something stuck in my psyche. I don't know what to think. With each song I hear about heartache, despair and relationships, I'm really at that point of questioning my life again. Is it now complete, or is it just at its starting point? On the other hand, do I just miss being in a relationship—a good one?

The past few weeks have gone by rather quickly. For today I am 49 years old. Yes, it's September 1, 2010, and I woke up early to begin my day. I'm not sure how I feel; I don't feel any older. Although I feel I have reached another milestone in my life. I have survived another birthday without my ex living in the same home as me. Tonight, I will celebrate with my son at dinner. Last year at this time, I was still hurting. I had so many evil thoughts about my ex and how we were only three weeks from becoming an "ex" couple. I wondered what he was feeling, what he was doing with "her," and how I would make it on my own. Today, I have persevered further down that path of divorce than I thought I could make it. I have more self-confidence, although I still have my moments of self-doubt. I still wonder how I will make it by myself, and then I wonder who is waiting to be a major part of my life. Like my ex used to say, "I've got the world by the balls, and I want to swing!" Yeah, he really did say that. I didn't know then what he meant by those words, but I think I know now. I really think that his desire was to be powerful, which seems to have pulled him away from his faith in God. I think he convinced himself that he needs to be absent from the man upstairs and only then he will be successful. To me, that's a scary fate. I don't know about anyone but me, because I would be lost without a guidance that keeps me on the straight and narrow. I don't think I would be complete and have gotten as far as I have without "his" guidance in my life. I have gotten closer to my faith since my divorce and my sense of calm has come back full force. I guess there was a gap in my life that now has been filled; for I can always pray for that guidance I so desperately need. Believe me, my prayers have been answered during this past year. My sorrow has lessened, my heart is still healing, and my direction has a very large arrow pointing towards my accomplishments.

Well, I have made it through another birthday without my ex. I'm not sure if it's getting easier or not doing things by myself. Just when I think I've made it over that hurdle, another one seems to pop up. I even wonder why people are so emotionally detached after being on their own for so long. Sometimes when you date someone who has been divorced, you have that sense of aloofness with him or her. Has their silence become their strength? Hello? Is anyone in that shell of a human? Maybe I'm just a person who will spill their guts too easily—here's another one of my weaknesses! I'm not sure which is easier, keeping all your emotions to yourself, or committing diarrhea of the mouth. I guess I just talk too much, but which is better, getting your emotions out of your soul, or leaving them there to rot? I guess you're damned if you do and damned if you don't! I just know that this past year has been the toughest lesson I've ever faced, and just think, there's the rest of my life to deal with now. Yippee!!

Now, I'm just baulking at life I guess, but I need that warmth of someone who wants to be near me. I guess that "loneliness" gene is never far away, huh? I guess it takes a major event, such as a birthday, death, or in my case the anniversary of a divorce to make your eyes open and make you examine where you're headed. Emotionally I'm tired and a little sad about the events that led me to this point in my life. I think I still feel vulnerable to this day. Up until this point, I've made it without too much trauma and aftereffects, but that anniversary is fast approaching. I guess I've only let others see a side of me, which I allow—the strong side. It's that region which portrays my strength and ambition for life. If they only knew that I am just as vulnerable as the next divorcee in that long line.

Today is Friday, September 3, 2010. Here is one more holiday (Labor Day) for me to celebrate as a divorcee. I have most of the weekend to myself, so I can keep busy with more updating to my townhouse. I want to have fun, but there are no plans for that now. I also want to have a housewarming party in a few weeks, and I must plan that event.

Keeping busy with the chores I planned hasn't stopped my mind from racing. For, I think I have finally found an answer why my marriage broke apart. I've wanted answers for so long now, and this morning at church I felt it was handed to me on a silver platter. Well, when a marriage goes array, God is not involved, and an impossible situation really is impossible. Say what? Well, the paster explained how he and his wife almost got a divorce after four years of marriage. His early family life was filled with violence and torment, and he took these actions into his married life. It wasn't until several months had passed and he had divorce papers in his hand, but he found the peace he needed with God's help.

He also mentioned that when a man commits adultery; he first commits it in his thoughts. Then when he is presented with the opportunity to cheat, he has accepted in his heart that it is ok to proceed with his actions. Wow! What a rush I got when I heard those words. I truly know that I will never get an apology from my ex now— for he has forgiven himself and only himself and my feelings don't and never will count. He will never realize that the feelings of others are just as important as his own. What has manufactured in his thought life can produce an instability that will never change unless he wants it to change. Unless he sees his actions as being "wrong," he will mentally and physically see them as something that is ok to do.

It's now September 9, 2010; it's exactly 14 days from that "D day" anniversary. I'm still not sure how I'm feeling. There's an emptiness that still exists in my soul and it's deep down. I even feel that I'm out of words to describe my thoughts. How does life get to this point and where do we go from here? I guess it's like being in the minor leagues (when you're single), and then you move to the major leagues after you have found your soul mate. Afterwards, your soul mate leaves you for another, so now you're back in the minor leagues again. Then, you're starting all over again with little or nothing like you did when you first met. All those memories, furniture, and stuff you accumulated together aren't important anymore. Someone put a tag on them to be donated to charity because they weren't needed. What? Someone did this without you asking and without your permission!

Talking about having permission. Now, I have another friend whose husband is fooling around. Just think she's at the point I was just over a year ago. As I talked with her the other day, she stated that her emotions were like a roller coaster. Boy, that rings a bell—more than she will know. She currently has no plans for her future even though this happened over three weeks ago. In addition, she's so scattered that her thoughts are all over the board. I know her pain and truly understand where she is currently in her life. I told her that I was here for her, she truly deserves to have a friend and now! The man she thought she knew has changed her forever. His actions will now affect more people than he can realize.

I still don't get why people cheat. Do they not realize that their actions create a domino effect so tall and wide that it takes down everything and everyone in its path? From now on, life will never be the same and trusting again will always be the "black mark" in the back of our minds. Jumping into the next relationship will always present us with doubts and second thoughts. I just know that the one-year anniversary of my divorce is just over a week away, and I'm not sure what I will think then. Then, about two weeks after that will be the anniversary of my marriage 20 years ago. I'm still, in some ways, considered an infant in this situation called divorce. However, I am treading water, and I can still breathe. The knots in my stomach are going away, and the feelings of sadness are lessening. Now, whether I will heal entirely is up to me, and whom I let in my life will be my decision. I can control some things, but not everything. I must survive.

So, do we get to the point in a relationship where our roots are so deep that we don't have wings to fly away when it is so wrong? Or do we want to hide so far away from our troubles that we want to fly south for the winter? Either way our emotions can consume our every thought. If we let life engulf us to the point of no return, we can never move forward like we should, right? Each anniversary of the day "he" left, the day "he" cheated, birthdays, holidays, etc., will always haunt us if we let it. Our goals in life must now take priority.

Looking after myself has to be a priority now that almost one year has passed. Freedom is at my fingertips, or is it? Will it be a great life to look forward to if I don't weaken? Plus, it's now September 16, 2010—just one more week until "that" anniversary. The emotions are still there to haunt me. Have I moved on? Am I used to being on my own for good? Gee, I hope not. I mean, life is meant for sharing with that special person, being alone is not what I want. Life around me is still moving in circles like a merry-go-round, so I need to jump on and enjoy the ride. I cannot look back and feel regret for "his" indiscretions. I still have my pride and my sense of morals; even though he washed his down the toilet. I cannot dwell on his successes or failures for it would devastate me—or would it? At this point, it doesn't matter because I keep seeing relationships falling apart all around me—three in the last month. It's as if that tragedy happened to me a very long time ago, but only a year has passed.

I have grown immensely over these past months. My trials and tribulations have made me stronger. It's as if I were learning to walk all over again. Getting up after falling time and time again just made me more determined to put one foot in front of the other and take those adventurous steps. Thinking about it, a child will strive to walk even though they fall time and time again. They cry, they look sad, but their determination is still there, and eventually they succeed. I guess this is how life should be viewed?

At this point in time we must decide whether we will reconcile (to some point) with our ex-spouse or continue to hate them forever. That's easier said than done. Besides, do we rationalize our actions if we don't forgive them, and then justify our actions against them by the depth of our hurt? Wow, who just said that? Isn't life about seeking and restoring our damaged relationship if we lift the burden from our hearts? I guess it requires being humble towards that person who created the grief in the first place—well, in our minds anyway. So just remember, if you're not willing to be "for" yourself, then you have made your decision to be against "yourself." Life is about goals and ambition, right? It's almost like what doctors say about older people, if you don't keep your brain active, you've then you have given up. As the Pastor said this weekend at church, "We are not guaranteed tomorrow!" If you condemn yourself from others' views, you have condemned yourself if you worship material things versus the main man upstairs—you know, God.

It's now September 20, 2010; just two more days and the one-year anniversary of my divorce will be here. This morning, I had a knot in my stomach just thinking that this day is almost upon me. Will he remember too and then celebrate? Well, why should I care? I just wonder if my son will remember, but if he does, we will discuss his feelings. I just know one thing; I will not condemn myself from his views about me, and our train wreck of a marriage that ended so badly. I know that every action starts with a thought—whether it is bad or good, those roots develop after a seed has been sowed. Once the roots are established, the blooms of consideration are present, actions are played out, and the responsibility of discretion is thrown out the window. Blaming others for our own actions and not taking responsibility for them is such a norm nowadays. For our children to thrive in this world, we must teach them responsibility and consequences, or they will repeat our mistakes. I don't want my son to repeat the sins of his father, nor do I want him to repeat my behavior and what I did when I found out about his father's cheating ways. I also don't want my son to blame his parents, when he becomes an adult, on his upbringing, if he fails in some way. We must all leave our problems behind—don't forget them, just learn from them and grow upward, not sideways. We must find that solution for us to continue growing and learning and not getting stuck in a sinkhole forever. Remember, trials in your life will come more often than you wish, but they will pass. It might take a while for it to "pass," but it will.

Just think, it's September 21, 2010—one more day and that "anniversary" will be upon me. Wow! Where did this past year go? I even made a comment to a co-worker yesterday that one year has almost passed since I got my walking papers, and she couldn't believe it had been that long. As the past few days have come and gone, I've realized that I got to this point in my life by shear determination and a lot of tears. Just think, the next 24 hours will bring that anniversary, and I will see it clearly.

Well, today is the day—September 22, 2010, has arrived! Do I feel any different? I guess I really don't know—besides, it's just Wednesday, right? Last year it wasn't just a "day," it was several hours of torment until 4:30 came which was the time given to the both of us to show up, take an oath to tell the truth, and to leave as separate individuals—not a married couple. It was just seven minutes after we both started speaking to the magistrate that we had ended our bond. So, are we both better off living separate lives? I truly believe we are, but I think we should have ended our marriage long before this. I guess it's different for everyone, for a person must be at a "done" point in his or her life to change direction. Today I don't feel remorse, nor do I feel a sense of loss. I do feel a sense of accomplishment and a powerful will to move forward and conquer my fears. I guess I really didn't know what I would think, but now I know there is a life after this "death" experience that I've felt for so long—and it is a good feeling.

I guess we all want to change direction at some point, and with that in mind, we need to plan on how to get there. It seems that our financial situation is our biggest hurdle to overcome. Do we stagger with that decision because we want to hold on, or do we realize that others will think badly about our choices? Whatever the reason to change direction, my advice to others is to think it through from the beginning to the end. Figure out the pros and cons and then decide if your decision will change your future to where you need and want to be. My decision to divorce was the right one to make, but for others getting a divorce may just be an easy way out. Just remember to follow your heart as much as you follow your mind—these two pieces of your life will serve you good if you let them.

My life was bent in so many positions for the past year; however, it was never broken. I have survived! For all who read this book and have gone through divorce, I wish you well in your spirit as well as in your life. You deserve happiness in every way!

www.ingramcontent.com/pod-product-compliance
Lightning Source LLC
Chambersburg PA
CBHW061758070526
44586CB00023B/2624